D1736089

Reforming the
Electoral Process in America

REFORMING THE ELECTORAL PROCESS IN AMERICA

Toward More Democracy in the 21st Century

Brian L. Fife

 PRAEGER

AN IMPRINT OF ABC-CLIO, LLC
Santa Barbara, California • Denver, Colorado • Oxford, England

Library of Congress Cataloging-in-Publication Data

Fife, Brian L.
    Reforming the electoral process in America : toward more democracy in the 21st century / Brian L. Fife.
        p. cm.
    Includes bibliographical references and index.
    ISBN 978-0-313-37227-8 (print : alk. paper) — ISBN 978-0-313-37228-5 (ebook)   1. Election law—United States—History.   2. Election law—United States.   3. Elections—Government policy—United States.   I. Title.
    KF4886.F544   2010
    342.73'07—dc22   2010007378

ISBN: 978-0-313-37227-8
EISBN: 978-0-313-37228-5

14   13   12   11   10   1   2   3   4   5

This book is also available on the World Wide Web as an eBook.
Visit www.abc-clio.com for details.

Praeger
An Imprint of ABC-CLIO, LLC

ABC-CLIO, LLC
130 Cremona Drive, P.O. Box 1911
Santa Barbara, California 93116-1911

This book is printed on acid-free paper ∞

Manufactured in the United States of America

To My Children—
Sam and Jack

And to a Generation of Their Cousins—
Alex, Anne, Emma, Hannah, Isabel,
Katie, Nick, Ryan, Samantha, and Tyler
Democracy is in Your Capable Hands

CONTENTS

TABLES

ACKNOWLEDGMENTS

I would like to thank all of my colleagues in the Department of Public Affairs and Policy at Indiana University—Purdue University Fort Wayne for their support through the years. In particular, I must recognize Jane Grant and Tammy Davich for their friendship and assistance in this project, and many others, for that matter. Mostly, I would like to thank my wife, Melissa, for imparting the democratic spirit on our children, Sam and Jack, as well as her first graders, through love, compassion, quality instruction, and random acts of kindness.

Chapter 1

HISTORY OF ELECTORAL REFORM EFFORTS IN AMERICA

When Alexis de Tocqueville initially visited the United States in the early 1830s,[1] he found Americans to be enthusiastic about voting. America was in the midst of the Jacksonian reform era that broadened popular participation in the electoral process.[2] Thus, a discernible tradition began in American history: the electoral process was reformed so as to make it more democratic and reflective of the collective wishes of the people.

The essential starting point in tracing the evolution of voting in America is to reflect on the debates waged on the subject by the Framers of the U.S. Constitution at the Philadelphia Convention in 1787. It is important to note, however, that the Framers were not unlike members of Congress today in that they were influenced greatly by the context of their time period. The vast majority of colonists were Caucasian, Protestant descendants of British citizens. The British were deeply entrenched in American history by 1787. The first permanent British settlement in America dated back to 1607 at Jamestown, Virginia. By the time of the American Revolution following the Declaration of Independence in 1776, there were 13 predominantly British colonies known as states.[3] Although there were clearly elite social groups in America at this time (e.g., northern merchants and southern plantation owners), most Americans existed as small subsistence farmers or in small farming villages. Though owning land was widespread, the elite still retained social authority.[4] Of utmost importance in appreciating the context of Philadelphia, however, is understanding the primary reason why the Framers ascended there in the first place. The Framers met and deliberated initially to discuss revising

America's first written constitution, the Articles of Confederation and Perpetual Union.

ARTICLES OF CONFEDERATION AND PERPETUAL UNION

The Articles of Confederation were written in 1777 and fully ratified by the states in 1781. Continental Congress delegates from all 13 states participated in the drafting of this governance structure, and noteworthy signers included Gouverneur Morris of New York; Robert Morris of Pennsylvania; John Hancock, Samuel Adams, and Elbridge Gerry of Massachusetts; and Roger Sherman and Samuel Huntington of Connecticut.[5] Contextually, the elites who wrote this constitution rejected the possibility of having a unitary form of government, where all power exists at the national level. The delegates clearly associated a unitary system with tyranny, which was their collective experience under British rule. Thus, they opted to create a confederal form of government. America's first experiment at home rule consisted of a confederation of sovereign states with a weak central government. Most political power, therefore, remained with the state governments.

The fledgling new confederation had no executive or judicial branch at the national level. The national government consisted of a unicameral Congress whose members were chosen annually by the state legislatures; each state, regardless of size, had one vote. After the Revolutionary War came to a successful end, it was quite apparent to many Americans that the Articles of Confederation were deficient in terms of promoting a prosperous domestic economy, creating a uniform foreign policy for the new nation, and for maintaining territorial security. Delegates to Congress were beholden to their state legislatures and narrowly pursued the perceived self-interests of the states involved, and there was a general absence of a collective sense of promoting the greater good of the nation. Some had concluded, prior to the Philadelphia Convention, that a stronger national government was needed to stabilize the new democracy. James Madison was a prominent advocate for a meeting in Annapolis, Maryland, in the fall of 1786. All states were invited to send delegates to Annapolis, but many state officials were fearful that the Annapolis Convention was a political ploy to undermine the Articles and the principle of state sovereignty. Only delegates from five states attended. Thanks to Alexander Hamilton, a resolution was passed that invited all states to send delegates to Philadelphia in May of 1787.[6]

An important event that occurred in Massachusetts in late 1786 and at the beginning of 1787 prompted more elites to question the plausibility of the existing Articles of Confederation. Americans experienced a postwar depression in the mid-1780s. Many farmers had considerable debt and their farms were heavily mortgaged. In Massachusetts, the state legislature was dominated by wealthy merchants who raised taxes repeatedly to pay off war bonds that those same merchants owned. The state printed no paper money, imprisoned debtors, and strictly enforced foreclosure laws. To stop the foreclosures of their farms and livelihood, desperate farmers under the leadership of Daniel Shays armed themselves and shut down county courthouses where their property was being foreclosed. Officials representing the Massachusetts government requested assistance from the inept Congress, to no avail. Thus, a mercenary army was hired and Shays' Rebellion was quelled with little loss of life.[7] As the Framers were convening in Philadelphia, they perceived that Shays' Rebellion was a much more menacing threat to their property interests as well as to social order than reality would have it. This perception would work to the political advantage of one of the Framers who came well prepared to promote the creation of a stronger national government, James Madison.[8]

In terms of voting, along with most other key issues, the drafters of the Articles of Confederation determined that voting would be a states' rights issue. Very little substance was enumerated by the delegates of the Continental Congress on the subject. Under Article V, the constitution builders stipulated that: "For the more convenient management of the general interests of the united states, delegates should be annually appointed in such manner as the legislature of each state shall direct, to meet in Congress on the first Monday in November, in every year, with a power reserved to each state, to recall its delegates, or any of them, at any time within the year, and to send others in their stead, for the remainder of the Year."[9] Those who drafted the Articles believed that the states were better equipped to address issues related to voting. This paradigm would be largely replicated in Philadelphia as well.

PHILADELPHIA CONVENTION

James Madison arrived in Philadelphia with an elaborate plan for reforming the fledgling American democracy. Having concluded that a confederal form of government was destined to fail, Madison, with the assistance of other delegates from Virginia, drafted elaborate plans on his ideal vision of a republican government. The resolutions became known as the Virginia Plan.[10] These ideas, which eventually culminated in the creation of a stronger national government, would be debated extensively in Philadelphia. Thankfully, there is one comprehensive account of all the debates in Philadelphia from the summer of 1787. It was crafted by none other than James Madison himself.[11] Madison's account is invaluable as the Framers chose to meet in secret and not provide the general public with information about their deliberations.

The decisions made by the Framers are reflective of the time period and dominant paradigms, perceptions, and political realities in the 13 states over 220 years ago. When the Framers approved the Constitution on September 17, 1787,[12] they clearly sought to avoid excessive democracy when it pertained to voting. The debates in Philadelphia suggest that the democrats were in the vast minority, and a limited extension of voting rights prevailed as a result.

The House of Representatives was referred to as "the first branch" in the Virginia Plan.[13] Some contend that the first major controversial issue in Philadelphia was deciding how members would be elected to the lower chamber in the legislative body. As is replete throughout the summer of 1787, there were many different perspectives on this matter. Some advocated selection of the first branch by state legislatures, while others promoted direct election by the people. Other ideas included allowing only white males with property the right to vote, while some delegates touted the notion that "the second branch" (the future Senate) should select members of the House. Ultimately, only white males with property could exercise the franchise when the republic commenced under the Constitution in 1789.[14]

EARLY REFORM MEASURES

Early in the history of the American republic, democratic reforms evolved in a series of waves. According to one historian, a first wave occurred from 1801 to the War of 1812. Reductions in property requirements were implemented in Maryland, South Carolina, and New Jersey, but similar efforts were defeated in Massachusetts, Rhode Island, Connecticut, and New York. In the western United States, only one new state, Kentucky, was admitted to the Union without a property stipulation for voting. The second wave ensued from 1815 to 1828 when Andrew Jackson was elected president. Property barriers to voting only remained formidable in Rhode Island, Louisiana, Virginia, and North Carolina. A third reform era occurred primarily in the South in 1829–1830, where voting became more democratized in Mississippi, North Carolina, and Georgia. Finally, sparked by the Dorr War in Rhode Island in the 1840s, a fourth wave resulted in several states that had not already done so ending all forms of property tests for adult white males. Though many other barriers to voting remained in place (e.g., residency requirements, registry laws, poll taxes, alien voting, and naturalization procedures), the electorate expanded during these early decades of the 19th century and resulted in a higher proportion of voters in the United States.[15]

Yet despite this ongoing period of reform in the voting process, two states (Rhode Island and South Carolina) still imposed property qualifications for voting by 1860. Thomas Dorr, a Harvard-educated attorney practicing in Rhode Island, became the leader of a popular movement to establish universal male suffrage. Rhode Island was still governed under a colonial charter established in 1663 that restricted voting to male landowners. In 1841 Dorr organized an extra-legal convention to frame a new constitution and abolish voting restrictions. The governor of Rhode Island declared that Dorr and his supporters were guilty of insurrection, declared a state of emergency, and called out the state militia to quell the insurrection. Dorr was arrested and found guilty of high treason against the state and was sentenced to a lifetime of hard labor. His harsh sentence was subsequently widely condemned, and he was pardoned and released in 1845. While the state adopted a new constitution and extended voting rights to native-born adult males and African Americans, it still imposed property requirements and lengthy residence requirements on immigrants.[16]

PASSAGE OF THE FIFTEENTH AMENDMENT

The Civil War amendments had a profound impact on American society in the aftermath of an unparalleled national crisis. The Thirteenth Amendment was ratified in 1865 and banned slavery forever. This amendment was the first measure designed to define the role of African Americans after the Union victory. African Americans were set free and would never again be enslaved. How much freedom African Americans would have vis-à-vis Caucasians was a question that would be addressed in subsequent years. An important partial response was provided in 1868 with the passage of the Fourteenth Amendment.[17] African Americans were given citizenship and equal protection of the law. Unfortunately, as history evolved this amendment was not consistently enforced, with profound implications on the evolution of civil rights in America.

The Fifteenth Amendment was the final step taken formally by Congress to define the place of African Americans in the post-Civil War era. Ratified in 1870, the Fifteenth Amendment stipulates the following:

Section 1. The right of citizens of the United States to vote shall not be denied or abridged by the United States or by any State on account of race, color, or previous condition of servitude.

Section 2. The Congress shall have power to enforce this article by appropriate legislation.

This amendment was the most controversial of the three. It did not un-equivocally declare that all adult African American males have the right to vote. The amendment instead is ambiguous, and it proved difficult to enforce. Once Reconstruction of the South ended in 1877 following the controversial 1876 presidential election,[18] a series of barriers was estab-lished in order to disenfranchise African Americans, including grandfa-ther clauses, literacy tests, poll taxes, white primaries, and overt violence. These efforts to deny African Americans the right to vote took genera-tions to correct. Many historians contend that the remaining barriers to the franchise based on race were not formally terminated until 1965 with the passage of the Voting Rights Act, 95 years after ratification of the Fifteenth Amendment.[19]

Accounts of the background, debate, passage, and ratification of the Fif-teenth Amendment are rich in details and illustrate the nature of history in general.[20] History is an interpretation of events that have already occurred, understanding that individual scholars may place a different emphasis on certain events in order to gain a broad understanding of the phenomena of interest. Clearly, Republican party leaders were largely responsible for pas-sage of the Civil War amendments.[21] Of all votes cast in the Senate pertain-ing to the Fifteenth Amendment, Republicans supported an equality policy for African Americans 70 percent of the time. By contrast, Democratic senators voted against the Fifteenth Amendment 77 percent of the time. In the House of Representatives, the proportions were similar. Republican House members voted in favor of roll call votes on the Fifteenth Amend-ment 85 percent of the time, whereas Democrats opposed the amendment 86 percent of the time.[22] However, ascertaining the motivations of promi-nent Republicans at the time is something that historians have debated for generations:

> In the past, historians have recognized the importance of the Republican party in passing these measures, but they have sharply disagreed over the motivations of Republican congressmen. Whether condemning or praising the amendments, most historians have more often than not attributed their passage to cynical or selfish motives. They have usually emphasized practical political considerations as the prime motive; the Republican party hoped to remain in power by a careful exclusion of southern white voters and a provi-sion of civil and political protection for the Negro. The Negro, once freed from slavery, was to be given constitutional protection in the areas of citi-zenship, laws and the franchise, in order to balance the power of the south-ern whites and thereby insure continued political power for the Republican party. Other historians have stressed economic gain—the establishment of Northern industrial power and control over all the nation—as the most im-portant motive. Radical leaders were said to be motivated by economic ends

(as well as political in some cases); they sought to link exclusion of the South with protection of the Negro in order that "the new industrial order which the Northeast was developing, would be safe." Some historians have emphasized moral idealism as the driving force behind the amendments. They contend that efforts had been made from the 1830s on to free the Negro and give him equality in its fullest sense and that the amendments were the final result of these efforts. Finally, a few historians have stressed the fusion of principle and expediency as the most logical explanation of the passage of these amendments.[23]

There are obviously many competing theories pertaining to why the Republicans promoted and successfully added the Fifteenth Amendment to the federal constitution. Understanding that the intuitive appeal of competing theories has not rendered a definitive conclusion regarding the motivation of the Republicans from 1865–1870 concerning suffrage for African American men, one point can be sustained. Though the full promise of the Fifteenth Amendment would take almost a century to be implemented, it was an important extension of civil liberties in a time of significant strife and turmoil in American political history.

PASSAGE OF THE NINETEENTH AMENDMENT

For two days in the summer of 1848, about 300 people, including 40 men, made history in Seneca Falls, New York.[24] Elizabeth Cady Stanton drafted the Declaration of Sentiments. In the Declaration, Ms. Stanton decreed that: "We hold these truths to be self-evident; that all men and women are created equal; that they are endowed by their Creator with certain inalienable rights; that among these are life, liberty, and the pursuit of happiness; that to secure these rights governments are instituted, deriving their just powers from the consent of the governed."[25] Stanton offered two substantive assertions with regard to suffrage for American women: "Having deprived her of this first right of a citizen, the elective franchise, thereby leaving her without representation in the halls of legislation, he has oppressed her on all sides."[26] To this, she further opined: "Now, in view of this entire disfranchisement of one-half the people of this country, their social and religious degradation, in view of the unjust laws above mentioned, and because women do feel themselves aggrieved, oppressed, and fraudulently deprived of their most sacred rights, we insist that they have immediate admission to all the rights and privileges which belong to them as citizens of these United States."[27]

Ms. Stanton's egalitarian philosophy was clearly not in sync with societal and cultural mores in America during the middle of the 19th century. In 1848, the primary objective in life for Caucasian women was marriage and family. Very few women worked for wages during this era; some young, unmarried women worked in textile mills, while others taught school or engaged in some form of domestic service. The chief occupation for most American women was to be a wife, mother, and homemaker. Laws reinforced this reality. Until the mid-1800s, married women could not own property. Most were barred from many professions, including law and medicine, until the latter part of the 19th century. Until the early 1900s, women could not vote or hold public office.[28]

In fact, women were put on a paternalistic, oppressive, and self-serving pedestal by some men during the 19th century. An illustration of this societal reality can be extracted from a very important, and unfortunate, U.S. Supreme Court ruling in 1873. In the case of *Bradwell v. Illinois*,[29] Myra Bradwell asserted that she had a right to practice law in Illinois by virtue of her status as a U.S. citizen. The state of Illinois had a law at the time that stipulated that only men could practice law in the state's courts. By an eight to one vote, the justices of the High tribunal affirmed the judgment of the Illinois Supreme Court. Bradwell argued that the privileges and immunities clause of the Fourteenth Amendment protected her right to practice law. Neither the judges of the Illinois Supreme Court or the justices of the federal Supreme Court agreed. The lone dissenter was Chief Justice Salmon P. Chase, though we do not know why because he never filed an opinion to explain his reasoning. He died a short time after the Court's justices held conference for the case.[30]

The associate justices serving at the time included Nathan Clifford, Noah Swayne, Samuel Miller, David Davis, Stephen Field, William Strong, Joseph Bradley, and Ward Hunt. Justice Bradley wrote a separate concurring opinion, joined by Justices Field and Swayne. Justice Bradley opined that:

> It certainly cannot be affirmed, as an historical fact, that this has ever been established as one of the fundamental privileges and immunities of the sex. On the contrary, the civil law, as well as nature herself, has always recognized a wide difference in the respective spheres and destinies of man and woman. Man is, or should be, women's protector and defender. The natural and proper timidity and delicacy which belongs to the female sex evidently unfits it for many of the occupations of civil life. The Constitution of the family organization, which is founded in the divine ordinance as well as in the nature of things, indicates the domestic sphere as that which properly belongs to the domain and functions of womanhood. The harmony, not to say identity, of interest and views which belong, or should belong, to the family institution is repugnant to the idea of a woman adopting a distinct and independent career from that of her husband. So firmly fixed was this sentiment in the founders of the common law that it became a maxim of that system of jurisprudence that a woman had no legal existence separate

from her husband, who was regarded as her head and representative in the social state, and, notwithstanding some recent modifications of this civil status, many of the special rules of law flowing from and dependent upon this cardinal principle will exist in full force in most states. One of these is that a married woman is incapable, without her husband's consent, of making contracts which shall be binding on her or him. This very capacity was one circumstance which the Supreme Court of Illinois deemed unimportant in rendering a married woman incompetent fully to perform the duties and trusts that belong to the office of an attorney and counselor. It is true that many women are unmarried and not affected by any of the duties, complications, and incapacities arising out of the married state, but these are exceptions to the general rule. The paramount destiny and mission of woman are to fulfill the noble and benign offices of wife and mother. This is the law of the Creator. And the rules of civil society must be adapted to the general constitution of things, and cannot be based upon exceptional cases.[31]

Yet some progress was witnessed in the states with regard to extending the franchise to women in state and local offices, particularly in the western United States. The Wyoming Territory enfranchised women voters in 1869, followed by Utah in 1870 and Washington in 1883.[32] Some historians contend that demography may have been a primary reason why suffrage for women occurred in the West before any other region of the country. Simply put, women were needed to help develop the frontier. Wyoming had a six to one ratio of men to women. Wives and children were in short supply, whereas in the eastern United States, men were relatively scarce due to the heavy loss of life during the Civil War. Thus, some legislators felt that suffrage would prompt more women to emigrate to the West, which would help in balancing gender ratios and therefore permit for the growth in families as well.[33]

Other historians contend that women won the vote in the western states due primarily to mobilization and structural opportunities. In terms of mobilization, state suffrage movements were successful when they actively raised funds for their cause and where they framed rationales for suffrage in ways that did not offend traditional beliefs about the proper role of women in American society. In terms of structural issues, suffrage movements prevailed when the procedural steps involved in expanding the franchise to women were relatively few and simple and where the major political parties endorsed suffrage. Also, the suffragists were victorious where gendered opportunities meant that women were already moving into male domains, particularly in higher education and in various professions. This blurring of male and female gender roles presumably made legislators and people more tolerant of supporting a woman's right to vote.[34] At the federal level, a constitutional amendment was proposed in 1878 stipulating that: "The right of citizens to vote shall not be abridged by the United States or by any State on account of sex."[35] The same amendment would be introduced in every session of Congress for the next 41 years. Ironically, the amendment that would pass Congress in 1919 was only altered incrementally.

Though women gained the franchise in several states already, progress was notoriously slow at the national level. In the second decade of the 20th century, however, a series of contextual events facilitated the passage and ratification of the Nineteenth Amendment. In 1912, Theodore Roosevelt's Progressive (Bull Moose) Party became the first national political party to endorse suffrage for women: "The Progressive Party, believing that no people can justly claim to be a true democracy which denies political rights on account of sex, pledges itself to the task of securing equal suffrage to men and women alike."[36]

In the fascinating 1912 presidential election, three significant contenders sought the presidency: the incumbent Republican, William Howard Taft; the Democratic challenger, Woodrow Wilson; and the Progressive challenger, former Republican President Theodore Roosevelt, who held office from 1901–1909. Mr. Roosevelt unsuccessfully challenged President Taft for the Republican nomination after being out of office for one term; he finished runner-up to Mr. Wilson, who became the 28th president, while Mr. Taft polled a distant third.[37]

Theodore Roosevelt's personal views on suffrage for women were articulated in his autobiography, which was originally published in 1913. His theoretical views about women voting are candid and self-reflective and can be described as both democratic and republican in nature:

Suffrage for women should be looked on from this standpoint. Personally I feel that it is exactly as much a "right" of women as of men to vote. But the important point with both men and women is to treat the exercise of the suffrage as a duty, which, in the long run, must be well performed to be of the slightest value. I always favored woman's suffrage, but only tepidly, until my association with women like Jane Addams and Frances Kellor, who desired it as one means of enabling them to render better and more efficient service, changed me into a zealous instead of a lukewarm adherent of the cause—in spite of the fact that a few of the best women of the same type, women like Mary Antin, did not favor the movement. A vote is like a rifle: its usefulness depends on the character of the user. The mere possession of the vote will do no more benefit men and women not sufficiently developed to use it than the possession of rifles will turn untrained Egyptian fellaheen into soldiers. This is as true of women as of man—and no more true. Universal suffrage in Hayti has not made the Haytians able to govern themselves in any true sense; and woman suffrage in Utah in no shape or way affected the problem of polygamy. I believe in suffrage for women in America, because I think they are fit for it. I believe for women, as for men, more in the duty of fitting one's self to do well and wisely with the ballot than in the naked right to cast the ballot.[38]

It is important to note, however, that the Progressives had a broad view of women's rights. They did not simply focus on suffrage, but espoused the premise that women could be equal partners with men in a more profound manner.[39]

Although the Progressives nominated Theodore Roosevelt for president again in 1916, he declined the opportunity to run against Woodrow Wilson again and the Republican nominee, Charles Evans Hughes. Following the reelection of President Wilson, many leading Progressives, including President Roosevelt, formally returned to their former political parties. By 1918, Theodore Roosevelt was the most prominent leader in the Republican party again. He was favored to win his party's nomination in the 1920 presidential election, but he died in 1919, thus paving the way for the ascendancy of Warren Harding of Ohio.[40]

The man who defeated former President Roosevelt in the 1912 presidential election, Woodrow Wilson, would later support the suffragists when it became apparent that they were destined to prevail in their quest to amend the federal constitution. Some historians believe that Mr. Wilson was persuaded by the National American Woman Suffrage Association to support its cause and simultaneously pressured by the militant National Woman's Party, but they also contend that President Wilson's activism after 1918 in favor of the suffrage movement was primarily a function of his commitment to social justice.[41] Others maintain that the National Woman's Party stressed the inconsistency between Mr. Wilson's advocacy of democracy abroad and his indifference to democracy in the United States. The president was embarrassed by this opposition and attempted to manipulate the press and public opinion to thwart it. Having failed in his efforts, he announced his public support for suffrage in 1918.[42]

On May 21, 1919, the suffrage amendment passed the U.S. House of Representatives by a 304–89 margin. Under the U.S. Constitution, a two-thirds majority vote is required in both houses of Congress for an amendment proposal to pass, and then it must be ratified by three-fourths of the state legislatures. Seventy-seven percent of House members who voted endorsed suffrage. The proposal was later passed in the U.S. Senate on June 4, 1919, by a 56–25 margin (69% of Senate members who voted supported the proposal).[43] On August 18, 1920, Tennessee became the 36th state to ratify the Nineteenth Amendment.[44]

OTHER PROGRESSIVE ERA ELECTORAL CHANGES, 1890–1920

The Progressives[45] had a great deal of faith in the people; they felt that citizens wanted good government, and reformers sought to make changes in the structure of the American political system so that the people could directly rule. This ideology prompted them to pursue a number of different policies designed to enhance democratic rule. These include *inter alia*, suffrage for women, but also direct election of U.S. senators, the advent of the direct primary, the use of the secret (Australian) ballot, and the initiative, referendum, and recall.[46]

Passage of the Seventeenth Amendment

The Framers of the Constitution did not allow the people to directly elect U.S. senators. Under the original constitutional framework, U.S. senators were selected by their state legislatures. The Framers stipulated in Article I, section 3 that "the Senate of the United States shall be composed of two Senators from each state, chosen by the legislature thereof for six Years; and each Senator shall have one vote."

The Framers clearly desired and intended for the Senate to be insulated from public opinion. As the upper chamber in the legislative branch of government, the Senate was designed to include legislators who would be positioned to carefully debate the great issues of the day without direct pressure from the people. The Framers collectively avoided excessive democracy in the original Constitution because senators and presidents were not selected by the people directly (presidents are still directly elected by the Electoral College), leaving the House of Representatives as the most democratic branch at the national level and, therefore, directly affected and impacted by public opinion.

By the early 20th century, both the U.S. Senate and state legislatures were plagued by corruption, inefficiency, disorder, and the inability to address legislative business. The business of state legislatures was repeatedly stymied by opposing factions trying to elect or defeat nominees to the U.S. Senate. The failure of state legislatures to fill vacancies in the U.S. Senate meant that it oftentimes did not have a full array of senators. The people were most adversely affected, as their interests were not being addressed at both the state and national levels.[47]

In order to prevent corruption in the Senate, direct election of senators was first suggested in 1826. This idea was later articulated by Andrew Johnson in the 1850s and 1860s, particularly when he was a U.S. senator and then president when Abraham Lincoln was assassinated. Mr. Johnson was rebuffed in the Senate because few members of this prestigious institution were willing to abolish the very system to which they owed their legislative seats. This movement resurfaced in the 1880s and 1890s and became a plank in the Populist party program in every election after 1892. It was also in the Democratic party platform in every presidential election year between 1900 and 1912. The House of Representatives adopted a constitutional amendment calling for direct election of U.S. senators five times between 1893 and 1902; each time, the amendment died in the Senate. However, momentum for reform grew rapidly when influential members of the media, including the publisher William Randolph Hearst, championed the cause of direct election by utilizing muckraking articles. Mr. Hearst hired a veteran reporter, David Graham Phillips, who wrote very critical articles on senators and portrayed them as pawns of the wealthy and elite. These articles contributed to the galvanization of public opinion to pressure the Senate for reform. As a result, the Senate passed the Seventeenth Amendment on June 12, 1911, and the House subsequently did so on May 13, 1912. It was ratified by the requisite number of states in 1913 and was first implemented in the 1914 federal elections.[48]

The Advent of the Direct Primary

The Framers of the Constitution did not design a mechanism to nominate candidates for the political parties because parties did not exist in America at the time. By the 1800 elections, two major parties emerged: the Federalists, a party primarily organized by Alexander Hamilton, and the Democratic-Republicans, a party largely created by Thomas Jefferson. Candidates for president subsequently were nominated by King Caucus, meaning that congressional party leaders selected candidates to represent their respective party organizations. Both parties selected their presidential candidates in this manner in 1800 (Thomas Jefferson was the candidate for the Democratic-Republicans, and John Adams was the Federalist candidate). The Democratic-Republicans continued using King Caucus until 1824. The Federalists did so only from 1800 to 1808. While the Federalist party did field presidential candidates in 1812 and 1816, top party leaders, meeting in secret, selected their candidates.[49]

King Caucus was never replicated after 1824 for two primary reasons. First, the Federalist party ceased to be a viable political entity. Indeed, the Federalists never controlled the presidency, Senate, or House of Representatives after the 1800 elections. Second, Andrew Jackson was a staunch opponent to King Caucus. He viewed this system as corrupt and elitist, particularly since he lost the 1824 presidential election in spite of the fact that he won the popular vote (the members of the House of Representatives ultimately selected the runner-up in the popular vote, John Quincy

Adams). In 1828, nominations were very decentralized and state-based. Though it was cumbersome for candidates to unify diverse elements behind a single national ticket, Mr. Jackson succeeded and was elected to his first term.[50]

National nominating conventions supplanted King Caucus in terms of selecting presidential candidates. The first nominating convention was held in a saloon in Baltimore by the Anti-Mason party in 1831. In 1824, the once dominant Democratic–Republican party split into several factions. One splinter group was led by Andrew Jackson, and would later become the Democratic party. Democratic party members believed in the doctrine of states' rights. Another faction, led by John Quincy Adams and Henry Clay, was known as the National Republican party, which later became the Whig party. The Whigs supported a stronger national government, stronger defense, and internal infrastructure improvements. The National Republicans and the Democrats held their own conventions as well in advance of the 1832 elections. The nominee for the Democrats, the incumbent Andrew Jackson, wanted to demonstrate popular support for his presidency. He also wanted to ensure that Martin Van Buren would be his running mate. The Democrats held another convention in 1836; this time, it was to make certain that Vice president Van Buren would be President Jackson's successor as the Democratic nominee. The Whigs, however, did not hold a convention in 1836. They ran three regional candidates for president to run against Mr. Van Buren. All were nominated by the states. Martin Van Buren prevailed, and thereafter, the major political parties have held nominating conventions to select their candidates.[51]

Political parties were free to nominate candidates as party tradition, custom, or rules might provide. This system was not very democratic in that there was little to no citizen input. One account of this approach to fielding candidates for the general election was particularly strident in its scathing criticism: "The abuses that arose under a system that staked the immense spoils of party victory on the throw of a caucus held without legal regulation of any sort were numerous and varied. They ranged from brutal violence and coarse fraud to the most refined and subtle cunning, and included every method that seemed adapted to the all-important object of securing the desired majority and controlling the convention."[52]

In conjunction with other reforms during the Progressive Era, the people demanded more input into the nomination process. This concept was not new in the late 19th and early 20th centuries, as experiments with the direct primary had already been witnessed in Pennsylvania in the 1860s, and for many years it had been in use throughout the southern and western states. The theoretical essence of this movement was captured in this commentary:

The movement was in part a democratic one, and was animated by a desire for wider popular participation in government. In this sense it was a part of a broad tendency in the direction of popular control over all the agencies of politics. The referendum, the initiative, the recall, and the direct primary are organic parts of a general growth and democratic sentiment, demanding methods by which more direct responsibility of the governor to the governed can be secured. In the second place, the demand for the direct primary grew out of the general discontent regarding social and industrial conditions. The party system was regarded as an important element in these conditions, and popular opposition converged upon the convention as the source of much of the evil it was desired to eliminate. Startling disclosures respecting the betrayal of public trust by party leaders aroused the people to a crusade for responsible party government.[53]

Florida was the first state to provide its political parties with the option of holding primaries. In 1904, the Democrats conducted a statewide vote for convention delegates. The following year a law was passed in Wisconsin that permitted the direct election of delegates to nominating conventions. Other states replicated this practice, and by 1912, 15 states provided for some type of primary election.[54]

Former President Theodore Roosevelt was the first presidential candidate who sought to use primaries as a means to secure a major party nomination. About 42 percent of Republican delegates were selected in primaries in 1912. President Roosevelt won 9 out of 10 contested primaries against President Taft but still lost the nomination. The incumbent, Mr. Taft, had the support of regular party leaders who controlled the outcome of the nomination process. Partially as a reaction to the Republican nomination process in 1912, additional states adopted primaries. By 1916, more than half of the states held a Republican or a Democratic primary.[55]

It took primaries several decades to become firmly entrenched in the American electoral process. State party leaders did not like them because they viewed them as a threat to their own influence on electoral politics. Public participation in primaries was disappointing. Primaries generally resulted in participation from a small fraction of the electorate.[56] Primaries were not essential to securing the presidential nomination of either major party, and running in them was largely perceived to be a sign of weakness and not strength. With the possible exceptions of John Kennedy's victories in West Virginia and Wisconsin in 1960, primaries were not necessary for winning the presidential nomination until the 1970s.[57] In 1968, Hubert Humphrey (D-Minnesota) was the last presidential major party nominee not to run in any primaries. This was contextual in that Lyndon Johnson decided not to run for another term, Robert F. Kennedy was assassinated in June, and the party was deeply divided over the Vietnam War. Since

1972, primaries have become absolutely instrumental in the presidential nomination process.[58]

The Evolution of the Australian Ballot

The party ballot was used extensively by the mid-19th century in the United States. The party ballots were generally printed and contained the names of the candidates and the designation of the offices. The ticket of each party was separate and could be distinguished from other tickets as they were typically of a different color.[59] Because of this practice, there was no secrecy when it came to voting in America. In fact, voter intimidation was quite common at this point in history. Bribery was a fairly overt practice as well.[60]

Because of the lack of privacy and other realities associated with open voting, reformers in Australia sought to alleviate some of the deficiencies in their electoral system so that voting would be done secretly so as to reduce mob violence in their country. The secret ballot was first proposed in Australia in 1851 and implemented in 1857. The secret ballot, commonly known as the Australian ballot, includes the names of all the candidates representing the various political parties, for designated offices. Voter choices are confidential and political party leaders are unaware of the voter choices in a given election.[61]

The use of the Australian ballot spread to many European nations shortly after it became utilized extensively across the Australian territories, and it was first incorporated in the United States in Massachusetts in 1888. Within four years, all the American states adopted the Australian ballot for elections, making Grover Cleveland the first U.S. president elected completely under the Australian ballot in 1892.[62] The differences between the two ballot systems can be summarized in a succinct manner:

> The Australian ballot differed from the unofficial ballot in the following particulars: first, all ballots are prepared by state officials and none but the official ballot can be used in public elections; secondly, the manner by which candidates can be nominated is regulated by statute; thirdly, ballots are distributed only by sworn election officers stationed within the polling-place on the day of the election; fourthly, the form of the ballot is prescribed by law and all ballots are uniform in any precinct; fifthly, ballots must be marked by the elector in secret and deposited so that their contents cannot be seen; sixthly, the entire process of the preparation, casting, and counting of the ballots is regulated by statute, and any violation or abuse of this law can be corrected by an appeal to the courts. This judicial control is one of the great differences of the official ballot over the former system.[63]

The utilization of the Australian ballot permitted citizens to register their electoral preferences without fear of reprisal. Compared to the previous system, popular sovereignty was enhanced and the collective preferences of the people were more accurately depicted. The importance of secret voting was encompassed in a very important document after World War II. In the Universal Declaration of Human Rights, adopted by the General Assembly of the United Nations on December 10, 1948, the responsibility of government to ensure democratic elections is emphatically noted:

> The will of the people shall be the basis of the authority of the government; this will shall be expressed in periodic and genuine elections which shall be by universal and equal suffrage and shall be held by secret vote or by equivalent free voting procedures.[64]

Lessons from history are instrumental in improving the human condition. Reforming electoral procedures in the United States in order to promote a more vibrant democracy has been a recurring objective since the very infancy of the republic. History is replete on two fronts. First, efforts to promote fairness and the democratic ethos do not always succeed. The plight of many reform efforts in American history suggests that reformers are often met with initial failure in their quest to enhance popular sovereignty. Thus, reformers must typically be patient and enduring to experience the time when their ideas about politics and public affairs will be embraced and truly enacted into law. Second, reforming electoral procedures is a constant work in progress. Human enterprises are flawed by definition, at least to some extent, and electoral procedures are not unique in this regard.

The Initiative, Referendum, and Recall

During the Progressive Era, reformers sought to advance the cause of democracy at the state level by pressing state officials to adopt three modes of direct democracy: the initiative, the referendum, and the recall. An *initiative* is a petition, signed by a certain minimum number of registered voters, to compel a public vote on a proposed law, constitutional amendment, or ordinance. The initiative, referred to by some as "citizen lawmaking,"[65] may be immediately binding (a direct initiative) or first considered by the state legislature (an indirect initiative) before going into effect.[66] A *referendum* literally is a ballot question decided directly by the will of the majority. It occurs when the electorate is asked to accept or reject a proposal. Simply put, the majority determines the outcome of a given public policy. It is not uncommon for the popular press to refer to initiatives as referendums.[67] A *recall* election has been rarely used in American history and is a procedure that allows voters to remove an elected official from public office. Although this procedure received a great deal of national press coverage in 2003 when California voters recalled Gray Davis, the Democratic governor, and replaced him with Republican Arnold Schwarzenegger, it was only the second time in history that a state governor was recalled (the other being North Dakota Governor Lynn Frazier in 1921).

The ethos of the Progressive vision when it pertains to letting the people rule directly was captured by the eminent James Bryce, who had opposition to direct legislation,[68] over a century ago:

> As the republic went on working out both in theory and in practice those conceptions of democracy and popular sovereignty which had been only vaguely apprehended when enunciated at the Revolution, the faith of the average man in himself became stronger, his love of equality greater, his desire, not only to rule, but to rule directly in his own proper person, more constant. These sentiments would have told still further upon State governments had they not found large scope in local government. However, even in State affairs they made it an article of faith that no constitution could be enacted save by the direct vote of the citizens; and they inclined the citizens to seize such chances as occurred of making laws for themselves in their own way. Concurrently with the growth of these tendencies there had been a decline in the quality of the State legislatures, and of the legislation which they turned out. They were regarded with less respect; they inspired less confidence. Hence the people had the further excuse for superseding the legislature, that they might reasonably fear it would neglect or spoil the work they desired to see done. And instead of being stimulated by this distrust to mend their ways and recover their former powers, the State legislatures fell in with the tendency, and promoted their own supersession. The chief interest of their members, as will be explained later, is in the passing of special or local acts, not of general public legislation. They are extremely timid, easily swayed by any active section of opinion, and afraid to stir when placed between the opposite fires of two such sections. Hence they welcomed the direct intervention of the people as relieving them of embarrassing problems.[69]

Both Theodore Roosevelt and Woodrow Wilson believed that the initiative in particular could serve as a check on unresponsive state legislatures. If legislators failed to heed the wishes of the citizenry, then the people could pass initiatives to either amend the state constitution or enact statutes themselves. In short, placing measures on the ballot allowed the people to circumvent state legislatures altogether if they believed that doing so would result in policies that promoted the greater common good.[70]

THE POLL TAX IN THE UNITED STATES

A poll tax is a capital tax levied equally on all adults. In the United States, the poll tax has long been connected with voting rights because officials in the southern states had utilized the poll tax to keep African Americans from voting. There are two distinct eras of poll tax requirements for voting in American history. Following the Revolutionary War, some states adopted the tax to substitute for property qualifications for voting. Gradually, the poll tax was eliminated by the mid-19th century. The second era began after the Civil War, when the poll tax was revived in the South after the ratification of the Fifteenth Amendment in 1870. This occurred primarily between 1890 to 1908.[71] Poll tax adoption during this time period in the former confederate states evolved in the following sequence: Florida, Mississippi, Tennessee, Arkansas, South Carolina, Louisiana, North Carolina, Alabama, Virginia, Texas, and Georgia.[72]

Poll taxes generally ranged from $1.00 to $2.00 per year. This amount of money was excessive to many poor African Americans and white sharecroppers, as neither rarely dealt in cash.[73] The purpose of the tax was clearly to disenfranchise African Americans and not to collect revenue because there are no records of any state officials prosecuting any citizens for failure to pay the tax.[74]

In 1937, a Caucasian man filed suit against Georgia's poll tax, alleging that it violated the equal protection clause and privileges and immunities clause of the Fourteenth Amendment and the Nineteenth Amendment's prohibition of discrimination in voting on the basis of sex. Women who were not registered to vote were exempt from the poll tax under Georgia's law.[75] The justices of the U.S. Supreme Court, however, did not endorse these arguments. Justice Pierce Butler wrote for a unanimous Court. He claimed that the Georgia poll tax was not designed to disenfranchise certain citizens. He also determined that the poll tax was a legitimate method for raising revenue. In his own words:

> The payment of poll taxes as a prerequisite to voting is a familiar and reasonable regulation long enforced in many states and for more than a century in Georgia. That measure reasonably may be deemed essential to that form of levy. Imposition without enforcement would be futile. Power to levy and power to collect are equally necessary. And, by the exaction of payment before registration, the right to vote is neither denied nor abridged on account of sex. It is fanciful to suggest that the Georgia law is a mere disguise under which to deny or abridge the right of men to vote on account of their sex.[76]

A movement to abolish the poll tax via a constitutional amendment ensued after the *Breedlove* decision in 1939. Such efforts were unsuccessful.

Though the use of the poll tax ceased in most states by 1960,[77] the Twenty-Fourth Amendment to the U.S. Constitution was ratified on January 23, 1964. The text of the amendment is as follows:

> Section 1. The right of citizens of the United States to vote in any primary or other election for President or Vice President, for electors for President or Vice President, or for Senator or Representative in Congress, shall not be denied or abridged by the United States or any State by reason of failure to pay any poll tax or other tax.
>
> Section 2. The Congress shall have power to enforce this article by appropriate legislation.

This amendment, however, was limited to federal elections. Officials in the commonwealth of Virginia, in anticipation of the promulgation of the Twenty-Fourth Amendment, eliminated the poll tax but replaced it with a provision whereby the federal voter could qualify to vote by either paying the customary poll tax or by filing a certificate of residence six months before the election. This law was invalidated by a unanimous Supreme Court in 1965.[78] Chief Justice Earl Warren wrote the majority opinion. In his ruling he emphasized the fact that prior to the proposal of the Twenty-Fourth Amendment in 1962, federal legislation to eliminate poll taxes, either by constitutional amendment or by statute, had been introduced in every Congress since 1939. This movement, according to Chief Justice Warren, was designed to eradicate overt discrimination:

> The Virginia poll tax was born of a desire to disenfranchise the Negro. At the Virginia Constitutional Convention of 1902, the sponsor of the suffrage plan of which the poll tax was an integral part frankly expressed the purpose of the suffrage proposal:
> "Discrimination! Why, that is precisely what we propose; that, exactly, is what this Convention was elected for—to discriminate to the very extremity of permissible action under the limitations of the Federal Constitution, with a view to the elimination of every negro voter who can be gotten rid of, legally, without materially impairing the numerical strength of the white electorate."[79]

The justices concluded that the poll tax was abolished by the Twenty-Fourth Amendment in federal elections, therefore nullifying the state action as it impaired the right to vote in federal elections.

Although the Twenty-Fourth Amendment came about more than a decade after the poll tax was a significant civil rights issue,[80] the amendment was based mostly on racial concerns rather than social class issues. In an important case in 1966,[81] several residents of Virginia challenged the state's poll tax. In a six to three decision, Justice William Douglas went beyond the issue of poll taxes to encompass economic realities as well. Justice Douglas reasoned that:

> We say the same whether the citizen, otherwise qualified to vote, has $1.50 in his pocket or nothing at all, pays the fee or fails to pay it. The principle that denies the State the right to dilute a citizen's vote on account of his economic status or other such factors, by analogy, bars a system which excludes those unable to pay a fee to vote or who fail to pay. It is argued that a State may exact fees from citizens for many different kinds of licenses; that, if it can demand from all an equal fee for a driver's license, it can demand from all an equal poll tax for voting. But we must remember that the interest of the State, when it comes to voting, is limited to the power to fix qualifications. Wealth, like race, creed, or color, is not germane to one's ability to participate intelligently in the electoral process. Lines drawn on the basis of wealth or property, like those of race, are traditionally disfavored. To introduce wealth or payment of a fee as a measure of a voter's qualifications is to introduce a capricious or irrelevant factor. The degree of discrimination is irrelevant. In this context—that is, as a condition of obtaining a ballot—the requirement of fee paying causes an "invidious" discrimination that runs afoul of the Equal Protection Clause.[82]

All nine justices agreed that poll taxes were contrary to the equal protection clause. Justices Hugo Black, John Harlan, and Potter Stewart believed that financial considerations for voting were not necessarily arbitrary and, therefore, did not fall under the general scope of the equal protection clause. According to Justice Black,

> My disagreement with the present decision is that, in holding the Virginia poll tax violative of the Equal Protection Clause, the Court has departed from long-established standards governing the application of that clause. The Equal Protection Clause prevents States from arbitrarily treating people differently under their laws. Whether any such differing treatment is to be deemed arbitrary depends on whether or not it reflects an appropriate differentiating classification among those affected; the clause has never been thought to require equal treatment of all persons despite differing circumstances. The test evolved by this Court for determining whether an asserted justifying classification exists is whether such a classification can be deemed to be founded on some rational or otherwise constitutionally permissible state policy.[83]

The dissenters were basically arguing that democracy should be expanded only through democratic means. It was up to Congress or the American people to adopt a new theory for democracy and not the federal courts.[84]

THE VOTING RIGHTS ACT OF 1965

President Lyndon B. Johnson signed the Voting Rights Act into law on August 6, 1965. The primary intent of the legislation was to codify the Fifteenth Amendment's guarantee that no person should be denied the right to vote on account of race.[85] The act immediately suspended literacy tests and other "devices" (including good character requirements and the need for prospective registrants to have a person vouch for them in states and counties where fewer than 50% of all adults had voted in 1964). The act also authorized the U.S. attorney general and federal examiners into the South to enroll voters and observe registration practices and procedures. The act further prohibited the governments of all affected areas from changing their electoral procedures without the approval of the civil rights division of the federal Department of Justice. State officials could only bring an end to federal supervision by demonstrating to a federal judge on the U.S. District Court for the District of Columbia that they had not utilized any discriminatory devices for five years. The act also included a finding by Congress that poll taxes in state elections abridged the right to vote.[86]

Literacy tests still had a very harmful effect on voting by African Americans in seven southern states in 1965: Alabama, Georgia, Louisiana, Mississippi, North Carolina, South Carolina, and Virginia.[87] Following his significant victory over Republican Barry Goldwater in the 1964 presidential election, the incumbent Democratic president, Lyndon Johnson, decided that he would pursue a voting rights statute. A number of contextual factors existed at the time. Previous civil rights laws did not deter white resistance to voting by African Americans. Public opinion on the issue was changing outside the deep South. Many Americans were abhorred by the brutality they witnessed on television on the part of some law enforcement officials in Alabama against African American demonstrators. In addition, President Johnson was captivated by the heroism exhibited by civil rights leaders at the time, especially Martin Luther King, Jr., and other activists who participated in the Selma campaign to secure equal voting rights for African Americans. President Johnson clearly understood that his place in history would partially be defined by his stance on voting rights, and he decided to lead the Democratic party on this issue even though he understood that it would result in an erosion in support of his party on the part of white southerners.[88]

Members of Congress extended Section 5 of the Voting Rights Act in 1970, 1975, and 1982.[89] With these extensions, Congress validated the Supreme Court's broad interpretation of the scope of Section 5. In *South Carolina v. Katzenbach* (1966),[90] the justices were asked to review the constitutionality of several provisions of the Voting Rights Act. Specifically,

South Carolina officials contended that the act violated states' rights to implement and control elections. The justices upheld the constitutionality of the act by an eight to one margin. Chief Justice Earl Warren, evoking the name and wisdom of Chief Justice John Marshall in his decision in *McCulloch v. Maryland* in 1819,[91] declared:

> After enduring nearly a century of widespread resistance to the Fifteenth Amendment, Congress has marshalled an array of potent weapons against the evil, with authority in the Attorney General to employ them effectively. Many of the areas directly affected by this development have indicated their willingness to abide by any restraints legitimately imposed upon them. We here hold that the portions of the Voting Rights Act properly before us are a valid means for carrying out the commands of the Fifteenth Amendment. Hopefully, millions of non-white Americans will now be able to participate for the first time on an equal basis in the government under which they live. We may finally look forward to the day when truly "[t]he right of citizens of the United States to vote shall not be denied or abridged by the United States or by any State on account of race, color, or previous condition of servitude."[92]

In 1982, Congress renewed the special provisions of the Voting Rights Act, as delineated in Sections 4–9, for 25 years. For the most part, extensions and amendments of the act have been bipartisan in nature.[93] This was also the case on July 27, 2006, when President George W. Bush signed Public Law 109–246 one year in advance of the 2007 expiration date.[94] The temporary provisions of the act were renewed for another 25 years.[95]

THE TWENTY-SIXTH AMENDMENT

Age resumed being an issue of contention among democratic advocates in the late 1960s during the zenith of student protests against the Vietnam War.[96] At that time, the legal voting age in all states except for Georgia and Kentucky was 21. Proponents of extending voting rights to 18, 19, and 20 year olds had succeeded first in Georgia (1943)[97] and then in Kentucky (1955)[98] due to a seemingly simple premise—if 18 to 20 year olds could be drafted into military service, engage in combat, and possibly lose their lives in service to their country, they ought to have the right to vote. At this time, however, women were not drafted and were not allowed to serve in combat forces if they enlisted in military service. Yet advocates of 18-year-old voting also emphasized other issues, especially during the 1950s and early 1960s. First, some asserted that the voting age should be lowered because contemporary young people were better educated than previous generations. Second, some contended that voting would channel the rising discontent of young people and result in a more positive mode of political participation for America's youth rather than campus demonstrations against the status quo. Third, others maintained that the same philosophical arguments utilized in the past with African Americans and women applied to young people as well.[99]

The members of Congress responded to public opinion regarding young people and the franchise in 1970. The Voting Rights Act of 1965 was renewed and amended to include a provision to lower the minimum age of voters in both state and federal elections from 21 to 18. Officials in Oregon challenged the constitutionality of the action by Congress on the grounds that states have the constitutional authority to establish criteria for voting, particularly in state elections.[100] In a five to four ruling, the Supreme Court justices determined that an 18-year-old requirement for voting is valid in national elections but not in state elections. Justice Hugo Black wrote the majority opinion:

> [T]he Constitution allotted to the States the power to make laws regarding national elections, but provided that, if Congress became dissatisfied with the state laws, Congress could alter them. A newly created national government could hardly have been expected to survive without the ultimate power to rule itself and to fill its offices under its own laws. The Voting Rights Act Amendments of 1970, now before this Court, evidence dissatisfaction of Congress with the voting age set by many of the States for national elections. I would hold, as have a long line of decisions in this Court, that Congress has ultimate supervisory power over congressional elections. Similarly, it is the prerogative of Congress to oversee the conduct of presidential and vice-presidential elections and to set the qualifications for voters for electors for those offices. It cannot be seriously contended that Congress has less power over the conduct of presidential elections that it has over congressional elections. On the other hand, the Constitution was also intended to preserve to the States the power that even the Colonies had to establish and maintain their own separate and independent governments, except insofar as the Constitution itself commands otherwise. My Brother Harlan has persuasively demonstrated that the Framers of the Constitution intended the States to keep for themselves, as provided in the Tenth Amendment, the power to regulate elections. My major disagreement with my Brother Harlan is that, while I agree as to the States' power to regulate the elections of their own officials, I believe, contrary to his view, that Congress has the final authority over federal elections.[101]

Essentially, Justice Black was writing for a majority of one—himself. Four of the justices (William Douglas, William Brennan, Byron White, and Thurgood Marshall) maintained that Congress had the proper authority to lower the voting age for both federal and state elections. Chief Justice

Warren Burger and three of his colleagues (John Marshall Harlan II, Potter Stewart, and Harry Blackmun), believed that Congress did not have the constitutional authority to lower the voting age in either state or federal elections. In this case, Justice Black's viewpoint prevailed in the outcome of the case.[102] This decision could have presented a very cumbersome administrative challenge to election officials in almost all of the states—the voting age for federal elections would have been different than state elections.[103] The decision in *Oregon v. Mitchell* was promulgated on December 21, 1970.[104] Due to the fact that many state legislators across America began to consider amending their state constitutions to lower the voting age to 18,[105] members of the 92nd Congress convened in early January 1971 and sought to place an 18-year-old vote amendment before the states.[106]

On January 25, 1971, Senator Jennings Randolph (D-West Virginia) sponsored a joint resolution that called for a constitutional amendment lowering the voting age to 18 in both federal and state elections. It was passed without dissent on March 10, 1971, with 94 affirmative votes. A companion resolution was introduced in the House of Representatives by Representative Emmanuel Celler (D-New York) on January 29, 1971. It was approved by a 400 to 19 vote on March 23, 1971.[107]

Since the proposed Twenty-Sixth Amendment achieved the required two-thirds majority under the Constitution, it was sent to the state legislatures for ratification. Even though many state legislators viewed the measure as an infringement on states' rights,[108] the Twenty-Sixth Amendment was ratified more expediently than any other constitutional amendment as the process was complete by July 1, 1971.[109]

NATIONAL VOTER REGISTRATION ACT OF 1993

The National Voter Registration Act (1993),[110] otherwise referred to as the Motor Voter Act, requires that citizens be allowed to register to vote while licensing their car, at social welfare offices, or by mail. It also prohibits the purging of voter registration lists except for a change of residency.[111] Advocates of this law contended that if registration procedures made it more palatable for citizens to vote, participation in elections would increase during an era of declining voter turnout in national elections.

The requirement of pre-election day registration was uncommon in most states until after the Civil War. Although officials in Massachusetts were registering voters as early as 1801, most antebellum proposals for registration systems were rejected as both unnecessary and overly partisan.[112]

Between the 1870s and World War I, officials in most states adopted formal procedures for voter registration. The rationale for this shift in election law was reflective of the time period. Voter registration, it was perceived, would help to eliminate fraudulent voting and would minimize volatile election-day conflicts at the polls.[113] During the Progressive Era, middle-class reformers strongly supported the requirement that citizens register in their states prior to exercising their right to vote. The Progressives believed that registration would limit political corruption during a time of urban political machines and boss politics.[114] The Progressives also had other objectives in mind with regard to their advocacy of voter registration. The Progressives sought to minimize the electoral strength of immigrants and African Americans as well. Unquestionably, the Progressives succeeded in this endeavor.[115]

Several important issues were germane to voter registration. Among some of the more prominent were the length of the registration period, its proximity to the date of an election, the size of the registration districts, the frequency of registration, the necessity of documentation of eligibility, and the location of the burden of proof. Not only were these critical details in the registration process, but they all had policy implications and were subject to conflict, change, and partisan strife.[116] Scholars have estimated that one-third or more of the decline in national voter turnout that occurred when registration systems were enacted can be attributed to the implementation of registration schemes and not for other reasons.[117]

Did the Progressives reduce fraudulent voting and assist in the process of political reform in the United States? Historians have debated this question for decades. There seems to be no definitive answer one way or the other. We do know that fraud and corruption during this time period did exist. Complaints about fraud emanated from a number of diverse sources. We also know that some of the claims of corruption were not factually based. Some historians have concluded that most elections were conducted properly where corrupt activities, when documented, were relatively few in number.[118] We also know that many of the reformers were openly antagonistic toward the poor, the working class, African Americans, and/or foreign-born immigrants.[119] Thus, Americans today still must scrutinize the decision-making process made by Progressives a century ago. Was corruption rampant in America at that time? Did the Progressives succeed in promoting democracy, even though the consequences were invariably harmful to the more indigent elements of society? Did voter registration laws promote more democracy in America rather than inhibit it?[120] These questions merit substantive analysis, as citizens in all states and the District of Columbia are still compelled to voluntarily register to be eligible to vote with only one exception as of this writing—North Dakota.[121]

Beginning in the 1960s,[122] election reformers attempted to dismantle registration impediments that had been established in the late 19th and early 20th centuries. In the decades that ensued, Republicans typically opposed efforts to revamp registration procedures such as registration by mail and same-day registration in the states on the grounds that they would increase fraud and that such registration methods would be expensive. Others contended that any federal law would be an unconstitutional intrusion on states' rights. Some rejected the notion that low voter turnout was problematic. Senator Mitch McConnell (R-Kentucky) argued that low voter turnout was a sign of a content democracy and that if more people were unhappy with the status quo, they would register and exercise their right to vote.[123] In the spring of 1992, Congress passed a motor voter bill, but President George H.W. Bush vetoed it for the aforementioned reasons. In 1993, President Bill Clinton signed a compromise bill into law after weeks of acrimony. The National Voter Registration Act passed by a 259–164 vote in the House of Representatives[124] and a 62–36 vote in the Senate.[125] Most of the affirmative votes were cast by Democrats, with only 20 Republicans in the House supporting the measure and 6 in the Senate. The measure took effect on January 1, 1995, and while it only applied to federal elections, it would obviously affect state and local elections because maintaining a separate registration system for nonfederal elections would be cumbersome and costly.[126]

A very important case was decided by the Supreme Court justices concerning registration procedures over 20 years before the National Voter Registration Act was signed into law. In *Dunn v. Blumstein* (1972),[127] a Tennessee law required a one-year residence in the state and a three-month residence in a county as a precondition for voting. In a six to one vote, the justices ruled that this law was an unconstitutional infringement upon the right to vote and the right to travel. Justice Thurgood Marshall penned the majority opinion; he was joined in his decision by Justices William Douglas, William Brennan, Potter Stewart, Byron White, and Harry Blackmun. Chief Justice Warren Burger dissented, and Justices Lewis Powell and William Rehnquist took no part in the consideration or decision of the case. The conflict arose when James Blumstein moved to Tennessee on June 12, 1970, to begin employment as an assistant professor of law at Vanderbilt University in Nashville. He attempted to register to vote on July 1, 1970, as he wished to participate in the August and November elections that year. The county registrar refused to register him as he did not meet the preconditions for voting under Tennessee law. After exhausting state administrative remedies, Blumstein challenged the constitutionality of the residence requirements. A three-judge federal district court was convened, and the judges determined that Tennessee's durational residence requirements were unconstitutional.[128]

The Court's majority affirmed the lower court ruling. Justice Marshall delineated the legal reasoning used by the majority:

In sum, durational residence laws must be measured by a strict equal protection test: they are unconstitutional unless the State can demonstrate that such laws are "necessary to promote a compelling governmental interest." Thus phrased, the constitutional question may sound like a mathematical formula. But legal "tests" do not have the precision of mathematical formulas. The key words emphasize a matter of degree: that a heavy burden of justification is on the State, and that the statute will be closely scrutinized in light of its asserted purposes. It is not sufficient for the State to show that durational residence requirements further a very substantial state interest. In pursuing that important interest, the State cannot choose means that unnecessarily burden or restrict constitutionally protected activity. Statutes affecting constitutional rights must be drawn with "precision," and must be "tailored" to serve their legitimate objectives. And if there are other, reasonable ways to achieve those goals with a lesser burden on constitutionally protected activity, a State may not choose the way of greater interference. If it acts at all, it must choose "less drastic means."[129]

Justice Marshall rejected the two primary arguments used by the representatives in defense of the Tennessee law. First, it was contended that the residence requirements ensured purity of the ballot box and thereby protected against fraudulent voting. Second, Tennessee state officials maintained that the residence requirements resulted in more knowledgeable voters who could exercise the right to vote in a more intelligent manner. With regard to the first argument, the justices ruled that registration up to 30 days before the election is reasonable in order to give officials time to prepare for the election. This standard is still intact today. A longer time period was not justified from the perspective of the Court's majority. On the second issue, Justice Marshall noted that the criterion of "intelligent" voting is elusive by definition and therefore susceptible of abuse.[130]

In dissent, Chief Justice Burger determined that a one-year requirement for voter registration was reasonable for newcomers to the state. To him, it was not substantively different than requiring children to wait 18 years before voting.[131] Thus, he defended the doctrine of states' rights in this electoral dispute highlighting the importance of federalism in the American republic.

HELP AMERICA VOTE ACT OF 2002

In the aftermath of a bitter presidential election in 2000,[132] where American citizens and people from across the world witnessed events on television evolve in Florida concerning the use of punchcard voting systems, members of Congress passed the Help America Vote Act of 2002[133] by a 357–48 margin in the House of Representatives[134] and a 92–2 vote in the Senate.[135] President George W. Bush signed the bill into law on October 29, 2002.[136]

The dispute between Al Gore and George W. Bush concerning the rightful winner of the popular vote, and subsequent Electoral College votes, was ultimately determined by the Supreme Court in *Bush v. Gore*.[137] Five of the justices ruled that the recount of votes that had commenced due to an order issued by the Florida Supreme Court should be stopped because it lacked uniform standards and thus violated the equal protection clause. This legal reasoning by the Court's majority was clearly unique and lacking in precedential value.[138]

The Help America Vote Act authorized the appropriation of $325 million[139] for the replacement of punchcard and mechanical lever machines[140] across the country. These two systems are more prone to error (i.e., unmarked, uncounted, and spoiled ballots)[141] than the other systems and were still widely used in 2002 when the act was made into law. The act authorized $3.9 billion to assist state officials in meeting new national standards for voting. In order to qualify for federal funds, state election administrators must take steps to give voters an opportunity to check their ballots for errors, provide at least one voting machine per precinct for disabled voters, define what constitutes a legal vote for each type of voting machine utilized in the state, create a centralized statewide voter registration base, and establish procedures where first-time voters must present a valid photo identification when registering. Voters who do not have a driver's license can instead provide the last four digits of their Social Security number. The act also permits citizens whose eligibility remains in question to cast a provisional ballot, which will not count until their eligibility is confirmed by local election officials.[142]

SUMMARY

The list of reform measures highlighted in this chapter is not meant to be exhaustive. Many policy changes have been implemented since 1789 with regard to voting and elections. The policies analyzed in this historical evolution collectively contributed to the expansion of democracy in America. It is important for the student of American politics to realize that the American democracy is a work in progress. Any human endeavor can be reformed or improved by definition. The manner in which elections are administered is certainly no exception. Thus, the discoveries and observations made by Alexis de Tocqueville about 180 years ago continue to have significant intrinsic value even today. He documented the expansion of the electoral process in the early 19th century. Contemporary democratic citizens who value the rights and responsibilities of the people in a representative democracy are truly engaging in the same activity in the context of the early 21st century.

Chapter 2

VOTING LAWS IN THE AMERICAN STATES

The Framers of the U.S. Constitution ordained that voting in the United States is an exercise in federalism. As stipulated in Article I, Section 4, "The Times, Places and Manner of holding Elections for Senators and Representatives, shall be prescribed in each State by the Legislature thereof; but the Congress may at any time by Law make or alter such Regulations." While the Framers permitted state officials to essentially create the rules governing their elections, members of Congress may intervene as they deem appropriate. In 1845, for example, Congress created a national election day for the first time.[1] Prior to this year, states were permitted to conduct their presidential elections any time during a 34-day period of time (before the first Wednesday in December) pursuant to a federal law passed on March 1, 1792.[2] Electing U.S. representatives on election day in every even-numbered year was established in 1875.[3] In 1914, it was decreed that U.S. senators would be selected on this date as well.[4]

An early November election date was selected by members of Congress for pragmatic reasons. In the mid-19th century, America was primarily an agrarian society. November was deemed by many to be perhaps the most opportune month for farmers to travel to the polls. The fall harvest was over, but in much of the country the weather was still temperate enough to traverse challenging roads. Because many rural residents had to travel a significant distance to the county seat in order to vote, Monday was not considered a viable option as many would have to begin their voyage on Sunday, which would have conflicted with church services and Sunday worship. Thus, Tuesday was selected. Lawmakers also wanted to ensure that election day did not occur on November 1 as this is All Saints Day, a holy day of obligation for Roman Catholics. Furthermore, members of Congress were cognizant that many business owners tallied their sales and expenses from the previous month on the first of each month. As such, legislators were collectively concerned that an unusually good or bad economic month might influence the vote if the election were held on the very first day of November.[5]

ELECTION LAWS IN THE STATES

The United States, as crafted in the U.S. Constitution, is a federal republic. When the Framers deliberated in Philadelphia, one stark reality at the time was the existence of 13 separate states. Consistent with a states' rights ideology when pertaining to elections, as well as sheer pragmatism in terms of traveling times, state officials had significant leeway in devising rules governing their respective electoral systems. This ethos is very much present today. A comparison of a number of state laws governing voting and elections captures a great deal of diversity between and among the states.

Voting Times on Election Day

Voting times on election day are depicted in Table 2.1. The polls are open the longest on election day in New York (15 hours), and polls are open for 14 hours in 4 states (Connecticut, Iowa, Louisiana, and New Jersey). Citizens are guaranteed by law to have 13 hours of voting time in 17 states: Alaska, Arizona, California, Delaware, District of Columbia,[6] Illinois, Maryland, Michigan, Missouri, North Carolina, Ohio, Pennsylvania, Utah, Virginia, Washington, West Virginia, and Wisconsin. Polls are open for 12 fixed hours in another 17 states: Alabama, Arkansas, Colorado, Florida, Georgia, Idaho, Indiana, Kentucky, Mississippi, Nebraska, Nevada, New Mexico, Oklahoma, South Carolina, South Dakota, Texas, and Wyoming. Citizens in Hawaii have 11 hours to vote on election day. Variance in polling hours, depending on jurisdiction as well as the discretion of local election officials, exists in another 10 states: Kansas, Maine, Massachusetts, Minnesota, Montana, New Hampshire, North Dakota, Rhode Island, Tennessee, and Vermont. The only state that does not have polling hours on election day is Oregon, as elections are conducted through the mail. Voting on election day ends the earliest in Hawaii, Indiana, and Kentucky (6 P.M.).

Table 2.1
Voting Times on Election Day in the American States (2009)

State	Polling Hours	Voting Time on Election Day
Alabama	7 A.M. to 7 P.M.	12 hours
Alaska	7 A.M. to 8 P.M.	13 hours
Arizona	6 A.M. to 7 P.M.	13 hours
Arkansas	7:30 A.M. to 7:30 P.M.	12 hours
California	7 A.M. to 8 P.M.	13 hours
Colorado	7 A.M. to 7 P.M.	12 hours
Connecticut	6 A.M. to 8 P.M.	14 hours
Delaware	7 A.M. to 8 P.M.	13 hours
District of Columbia	7 A.M. to 8 P.M.	13 hours
Florida	7 A.M. to 7 P.M.	12 hours
Georgia	7 A.M. to 7 P.M.	12 hours
Hawaii	7 A.M. to 6 P.M.	11 hours
Idaho	8 A.M. to 8 P.M.	12 hours
Illinois	6 A.M. to 7 P.M.	13 hours
Indiana	6 A.M. to 6 P.M.	12 hours
Iowa	7 A.M. to 9 P.M.	14 hours
Kansas	7 A.M. to 7 P.M.[1]	12 hours
Kentucky	6 A.M. to 6 P.M.	12 hours
Louisiana	6 A.M. to 8 P.M.	14 hours
Maine	6–10 A.M. to 8 P.M.[2]	varies by town
Maryland	7 A.M. to 8 P.M.	13 hours
Massachusetts	7 A.M. to 8 P.M.[3]	13 hours minimum[3]
Michigan	7 A.M. to 8 P.M.	13 hours
Minnesota	7 A.M. to 8 P.M.[4]	13 hours for most[4]
Mississippi	7 A.M. to 7 P.M.	12 hours
Missouri	6 A.M. to 7 P.M.	13 hours
Montana	7 A.M. to 8 P.M.[5]	13 hours for most[5]
Nebraska	7/8 A.M. to 7/8 P.M.[6]	12 hours
Nevada	7 A.M. to 7 P.M.	12 hours
New Hampshire	6–11 A.M. to 7–8 P.M.	varies by town
New Jersey	6 A.M. to 8 P.M.	14 hours
New Mexico	7 A.M. to 7 P.M.	12 hours
New York	6 A.M. to 9 P.M.	15 hours
North Carolina	6:30 A.M. to 7:30 P.M.	13 hours

(continued)

Table 2.1
Voting Times on Election Day in the American States (2009) *(continued)*

State	Polling Hours	Voting Time on Election Day
North Dakota	7–9 A.M. to 7–9 P.M.[7]	12 hours for most[7]
Ohio	6:30 A.M. to 7:30 P.M.	13 hours
Oklahoma	7 A.M. to 7 P.M.	12 hours
Oregon	none[8]	none[8]
Pennsylvania	7 A.M. to 8 P.M.	13 hours
Rhode Island	7–9 A.M. to 9 P.M.[9]	12 hours minimum[9]
South Carolina	7 A.M. to 7 P.M.	12 hours
South Dakota	7 A.M. to 7 P.M.	12 hours
Tennessee	7 A.M. to 7 P.M.[10]	12 hours for most[10]
Texas	7 A.M. to 7 P.M.	12 hours
Utah	7 A.M. to 8 P.M.	13 hours
Vermont	6–10 A.M. to 7 P.M.[11]	varies by town
Virginia	6 A.M. to 7 P.M.	13 hours
Washington	7 A.M. to 8 P.M.	13 hours
West Virginia	6:30 A.M. to 7:30 P.M.	13 hours
Wisconsin	7 A.M. to 8 P.M.	13 hours
Wyoming	7 A.M. to 7 P.M.	12 hours

[1] County election officials in Kansas can set different polling hours if the polls are open at least 12 consecutive hours. Polls can open no earlier than 6 A.M. and close no later than 8 P.M.
[2] Town election officials in Maine determine when polls open. The polls can be opened no earlier than 6 A.M. and no later than 9 A.M. on election day. In municipalities where the population is less than 4,000, the polls must be opened no later than 10 A.M. The closing time is fixed at 8 P.M., except in municipalities where the population is less than 100, where the polls can be closed after all registered voters have voted.
[3] The polls must be open from 7 A.M. to 8 P.M. in Massachusetts, but some town election officials may decide to open their polls as early as 5:45 A.M.
[4] In Minnesota, governing bodies of towns with less than 500 people may start voting at a later time but no later than 10 A.M.
[5] Polls must be open from 7 A.M. to 8 P.M. in Montana except where polling places have fewer than 200 registered voters. In such cases, polls must be open from 12 noon to 8 P.M.
[6] Polls in Nebraska are open 7 A.M. to 7 P.M. (mountain time) and 8 A.M. to 8 P.M. (central time).
[7] In North Dakota, most citizens vote between 7 A.M. to 7 P.M. Polls must be open no later than 9 A.M. and may be open until 9 P.M., depending upon the discretion of local election officials.
[8] Oregon is a voting by mail state.
[9] Town or city election officials determine when polls open in Rhode Island (most open between 7–9 A.M.) but all polls close at 9 P.M.
[10] Most polling places in Tennessee are open from 7 A.M. to 7 P.M. All precincts close at 8 P.M. eastern time and 7 P.M. central standard time. The polls must be open a minimum of 10 hours and a maximum of 13 hours. Local election officials determine when polls open.
[11] Local election officials determine when polls open in Vermont. All polls close at 7 P.M.

Source: League of Women Voters Education Fund. 2009. Voting in Your State. Accessed March 11, 2009, from: http://www.vote411.org/bystate.php.

Voter Registration

State laws governing in-person voter registration for general elections are presented in Table 2.2. Since the *Dunn v. Blumstein*[7] precedent (30 days registration in advance of election day) is still prevailing law even though computer technology has evolved since 1972, 33 of 51 state laws require a waiting period for voter registration of at least 20 days. Fourteen state laws require the full 30 days permitted by the justices of the High Court. Another eight states have waiting periods of 28 or 29 days. On the other end of the spectrum, citizens in Idaho, Iowa, Maine, Minnesota, Montana, New Hampshire, Wisconsin, and Wyoming have laws that permit same-day registration, that is, voters can first register and then vote on election day. Another nine states have registration requirements between 6 days and 15 days before the election. North Dakota is the only state that does not require voluntary registration, meaning that all residents are eligible to vote when they turn 18 years of age. At one time, mandatory registration was required in North Dakota. In 1895, the North Dakota Legislative Assembly enacted a bill requiring registration two weeks before every general or municipal election in cities or towns with a population of at least 1,000 people. Even with this requirement, unregistered voters could still appear at the polls and vote on election day by submitting an affidavit supported by the oath of a householder or registered voter attesting that the prospective voter was a resident and therefore entitled to vote. The registration law did not apply to primary elections, and at that time North Dakota was a strong one-party Republican state. Major electoral contests truly occurred in the June party primaries between Republican candidates and not in the general election between the Republican and Democratic nominees. In 1951, a bill that originated in the North Dakota Senate passed unanimously to repeal mandatory voter registration and left registration optional with the governing boards of the municipalities. It passed in the North Dakota House of Representatives by a 95 to 5 margin. Since that time, North Dakota Century Code (NDCC) Section 40–21–10 has provided for optional registration of voters within municipalities.[8]

Between 1957 and 1975, there were a number of attempts to pass legislation requiring mandatory statewide registration. In 1975, a bill requiring registration passed in the North Dakota House by a vote of 56 to 41 and 27 to 19 in the North Dakota Senate. The bill was vetoed by Governor Arthur Link, however.[9] Thus, elections in North Dakota have been conducted for about 60 years without mandatory registration.

Voter registration lists basically serve two purposes. The first objective is to ensure that only those citizens who are eligible participate in the electoral process and that they vote only once in each election. This is constructive

Table 2.2

In-Person State Voter Registration Laws for General Election Dates (2009)

Voter Registration Law	States with this Law	N
No registration required	North Dakota	1
Same-day registration	Idaho, Iowa, Maine, Minnesota, Montana, New Hampshire, Wisconsin, and Wyoming.	8
6 days before election	Vermont	1
7 days before election	Connecticut	1
10 days before election	Alabama	1
11 days before election	Nebraska	1
15 days before election	California, Kansas, South Dakota, Utah, andWashington.	5
20 days before election	Delaware and Massachusetts.	2
21 days before election	Maryland, Nevada, New Jersey, Oregon, and West Virginia.	5
25 days before election	New York, North Carolina, and Oklahoma.	3
27 days before election	Missouri	1
28 days before election	Illinois, Kentucky, and New Mexico.	3
29 days before election	Arizona, Colorado, Florida, Indiana, and Virginia.	5
30 days before election	Alaska, Arkansas, District of Columbia, Georgia, Hawaii, Louisiana, Michigan, Mississippi, Ohio, Pennsylvania, Rhode Island,[1] South Carolina, Tennessee, and Texas.	14

[1] Rhode Island General Law 17-1-3 allows a citizen who has missed the voter registration deadline to vote for president and vice president only at the local Board of Canvassers on election day.

Source: League of Women Voters Education Fund. 2009. Voting in Your State. Accessed March 11, 2009, from: http://www.vote411.org/bystate.php.

and is partly an artifact of fraudulent voting in the late 19th and early 20th centuries. The other objective is transparent and it is unjust. Voter registration has been used by those who control the administration of elections to make it cumbersome for their political opponents to exercise the franchise. Simply put, it has been used as a barrier to preclude certain groups from fully exercising their right to vote in a democratic republic.[10]

Laws requiring voters to register date back to 1801 in the commonwealth of Massachusetts, but voter registration was not the norm in the United States prior to the Civil War. Voter registration became commonplace across the states in the late 19th century. The burden of registration, therefore, shifted from the state to the individual. Between the Civil War and World War I, most states had formal laws requiring voter registration, at least in large urban areas.[11]

The explicit justification for the implementation of mandatory voter registration was to combat political fraud and corruption in American elections. During the time period in question, it was perceived that voter fraud was more common in larger cities, where many citizens were anonymous to local election officials. Typically, registration was required only in urban areas initially; in later decades mandatory registration would spread to rural America as well. An important motivation for election officials was not declared at the time: to impede the participation of groups deemed inferior and/or unsavory. In the north, voter registration laws were used to thwart working-class Americans and recent immigrants from southern and eastern Europe from voting. In the south, registration was particularly effective at disenfranchising African Americans.[12] It is important to understand the context of the times in which voter registration laws proliferated. While attempting to combat fraudulent elections during the period of corrupt urban political machines and boss politics, those advocating mandatory registration were clearly successful. Those desiring to reduce the electoral strength of African Americans and immigrants were also successful.[13] As a result of these laws, large numbers of eligible American voters numbering in the millions were kept from the polls.[14]

Early Voting

Pre-election day voting is permitted in 47 states; it is currently not a possibility in Maryland, Oregon, Rhode Island, and Washington. Included in Table 2.3 is a breakdown of early voting laws in the states. Existing statutes in 32 states allow for pre-election day voting either by voting on a machine or by an in-person absentee ballot. No excuse is required. The remaining 15 states (including the District of Columbia) have laws that permit citizens to engage in early voting, but they must provide an excuse, and voting is conducted through an in-person absentee ballot.

Absentee Voting

All the states and the District of Columbia have laws that allow for absentee voting. In a dichotomous manner, no excuse is required in 28 states for

Table 2.3
Early Voting Laws in the American States (2009)

Early Voting Law	States with this Law	N
Early voting permitted with no excuse required; in-person voting either by machine or in-person absentee ballot.	Alaska, Arizona, Arkansas, California, Colorado, Florida, Georgia, Hawaii, Idaho, Illinois, Indiana, Iowa, Kansas, Louisiana, Maine, Montana, Nebraska, Nevada, New Jersey, New Mexico, North Carolina, North Dakota, Ohio, Oklahoma, South Dakota, Tennessee, Texas, Utah, Vermont, West Virginia, Wisconsin, and Wyoming.	32
Early voting permitted; an excuse is required for in-person absentee voting.	Alabama, Connecticut, Delaware, District of Columbia, Kentucky, Massachusetts, Michigan, Minnesota, Mississippi, Missouri, New Hampshire, New York, Pennsylvania, South Carolina, and Virginia.	15
Early voting is not permitted.	Maryland, Oregon,[1] Rhode Island, and Washington.	4

[1] Oregon is a voting by mail state.

Sources: League of Women Voters Education Fund. 2009. Voting in Your State. Accessed March 11, 2009, from: http://www.vote411.org/bystate.php; and Early Voting Information Center at Reed College. 2009. Absentee and Early Voting Laws. Accessed March 16, 2009, from: http://earlyvoting.net/states/abslaws.php.

citizens to cast an absentee ballot. An excuse is required in the remaining 22 states and the District of Columbia. This dichotomy is depicted in Table 2.4.

"Time Off to Vote" Laws

State lawmakers have devised varied approaches to the issue of allowing workers to have paid or unpaid time off to vote on election day. The diversity of laws is summarized in Table 2.5. There are no existing statutes requiring time off to vote in 21 states. In the remaining states, up to one, two, three, or four or more hours are permitted, typically with a number of stipulations; others utilize a varied time allotment or simply have laws that prohibit employers from firing or threatening workers from taking a reasonable amount of time off of work to vote.[15]

Table 2.4
Absentee Voting Laws in the American States (2009)

Absentee Voting Law	States with this Law	N
Absentee voting permitted with no excuse required.	Alaska, Arizona, Arkansas, California, Colorado, Florida, Georgia, Hawaii, Idaho, Iowa, Kansas, Maine, Montana, Nebraska, Nevada, New Jersey, New Mexico, North Carolina, North Dakota, Ohio, Oklahoma, Oregon, South Dakota, Utah, Vermont, Washington, Wisconsin, and Wyoming.	28
Absentee voting permitted with an excuse required.	Alabama, Connecticut, Delaware, District of Columbia, Illinois, Indiana, Kentucky, Louisiana, Maryland, Massachusetts, Michigan, Minnesota, Mississippi, Missouri, New Hampshire, New York, Pennsylvania, Rhode Island, South Carolina, Tennessee, Texas, Virginia, and West Virginia.	23

Sources: League of Women Voters Education Fund. 2009. Voting in Your State. Accessed March 11, 2009, from: http://www.vote411.org/bystate.php; and Early Voting Information Center at Reed College. 2009. Absentee and Early Voting Laws. Accessed March 16, 2009, from: http://earlyvoting.net/states/abslaws.php.

Felons and the Franchise

Felony voting rights vary considerably by state.[16] Policies on felon voting can be categorized into four broad categories: (1) permanent disenfranchisement for all felony offenders; (2) permanent disenfranchisement for some felony offenders; (3) re-enfranchisement after completion of sentence, including parole and sometimes probation; and (4) states with minimal disenfranchisement.[17] Within these broad categories are six distinct approaches to dealing with convicted felons across the 50 states and the District of Columbia. These six differential policies are encompassed in Table 2.6. A citizen convicted of a felony in Maine or Vermont can cast an absentee ballot from jail while serving his or her sentence. If the same person commits the same crime in Virginia or Kentucky, he or she may never vote again unless voting rights are restored by official state action.[18]

Table 2.5
Time Off to Vote Laws in the American States (2009)

Time Off to Vote Law	States with this Law	N
No law requiring time off to vote.	Connecticut, District of Columbia, Delaware, Florida, Idaho, Indiana, Louisiana, Maine, Michigan, Mississippi, Montana, New Hampshire, New Jersey, North Carolina, North Dakota, Oregon, Pennsylvania, Rhode Island, South Carolina, Vermont, and Virginia.	21
Workers can take off up to 1 hour of work to vote.	Alabama and Wyoming.	2
Workers can take off up to 2 hours of work to vote.	Alaska, California, Colorado, Georgia, Hawaii, Illinois, Kansas, Maryland, Massachusetts, Nebraska, New Mexico, New York, Oklahoma, South Dakota, Utah, Washington, West Virginia, and Wisconsin.	18
Workers can take off up to 3 hours of work to vote.	Arizona, Iowa, Missouri, and Tennessee.	4
Workers can take off 4 or more hours to vote.	Kentucky[1] and Minnesota.[2]	2
Employers are required to create a schedule that permits all workers who desire to vote to have the opportunity to do so.	Arkansas	1
Time off varies depending on distance between work and polling site.	Nevada[3]	1
Employers cannot fire or threaten employees for taking a reasonable amount of time off to vote.	Ohio and Texas.	2

[1] In Kentucky, workers are allowed to take up to four hours for the purpose of voting.
[2] In Minnesota, workers are allowed to take the morning off for the purpose of voting.
[3] In Nevada, workers have between 1–3 hours time off to vote, depending on the distance between work and the polling station.

Source: Findlaw. 2009. State-by-State Time Off to Vote Laws. Accessed March 19, 2009, from: http://www.findlaw.com/voting-rights-law.html.

Table 2.6
Felon Voting Laws in the American States (2009)

Felon Voting Law	States with this Law	N
Permanent disenfranchisement for all felony offenders (unless individual rights are restored by the state)	Kentucky and Virginia.	2
Permanent disenfranchisement for at least some offenders (unless individual rights are restored by the state)	Alabama, Arizona, Delaware, Florida, Mississippi, Nevada, Tennessee, and Wyoming.	8
Voting rights restored upon completion of sentence, including prison, parole, and probation	Alaska, Arkansas, Georgia, Idaho, Iowa, Kansas, Louisiana, Maryland, Minnesota, Missouri, Nebraska[1], New Jersey, New Mexico, North Carolina, Oklahoma, South Carolina, Texas, Washington, West Virginia, and Wisconsin.	20
Voting rights restored after release from prison and discharge from parole (probationers may vote)	California, Colorado, Connecticut, New York, and South Dakota.	5
Voting rights restored after release from prison	District of Columbia, Hawaii, Illinois, Indiana, Massachusetts, Michigan, Montana, New Hampshire, North Dakota, Ohio, Oregon, Pennsylvania, Rhode Island, and Utah.	14
No disenfranchisement for people with criminal convictions	Maine and Vermont.	2

[1] Nebraska imposes a two-year waiting period upon completion of sentence.

Sources: Brennan Center for Justice. 2009. Voting After Criminal Conviction. Accessed March 20, 2009, from: http://www.brennancenter.org/; and Project Vote. January 5, 2007. Restoring Voting Rights to Former Felons. Accessed March 19, 2009, from: http://projectvote.org/.

In Alabama, Arizona, Delaware, Florida, Mississippi, Nevada, Tennessee, and Wyoming, people convicted of certain crimes are permanently disenfranchised; offenders in some states can apply for the restoration of their voting rights typically through a gubernatorial pardon.[19] In some states, voting rights are restored upon completion of a prison sentence, parole, and probation. In others, offenders are afforded voting rights automatically after release from prison and discharge from parole, meaning that probationers can vote. Other state laws result in the restoration of voting rights when a citizen is released from prison. According to officials from the Brennan Center for Justice at New York University School of Law, 5.3 million American citizens are currently not allowed to vote because of a criminal conviction, and 13 percent of all African American men have lost the right to vote, a rate that is seven times the national average.[20]

Voter Identification Requirements

Under the Help America Vote Act, all states are mandated to require identification from first-time voters who registered to vote by mail and did not provide proper verification of their identity with their mail-in voter registration. For all other voters, a person's sworn statement as to her or his identity is normally sufficient in order to vote.[21] Yet many states go beyond this federal act and require additional forms of identification in order to either register or vote.[22] Included in Table 2.7 are identification requirements by state specifically for voting.

Laws in 26 states require some form of identification in order to vote on a regular ballot. Statutes in the remaining 24 states and the District of Columbia do not require citizens to go beyond the federal standard delineated in the Help America Vote Act. In perhaps the most controversial Supreme Court case on elections since *Bush v. Gore*, the justices upheld Indiana's stringent identification law in April 2008 in *Crawford v. Marion County Election Board*.[23]

The legislators in the Indiana General Assembly enacted a voter identification law in 2005. The law required citizens voting in-person in either primary or general elections to present a photo identification to poll workers issued by the government. Promptly, the leaders of the Indiana Democratic Party and the members of the Marion County Democratic Central Committee filed suit in federal district court believing that the law was invalid and therefore sought to enjoin its enforcement.[24] The petitioners failed to meet their objective, however, as the statute was upheld in Federal District Court for the Southern District of Indiana and a divided panel of the Seventh Circuit Court of Appeals affirmed this judgment. Subsequently,

Table 2.7
Identification Laws for Voting in the American States (2009)

Voter Identification Law	States with this Law	N
Identification is required to vote on a regular ballot (more restrictive standard than policy created by the Help America Vote Act).	Alabama, Alaska, Arizona, Arkansas, Colorado, Connecticut, Delaware, Florida, Georgia, Hawaii, Indiana, Kansas,[1] Kentucky, Louisiana, Missouri, Montana, New Mexico, North Dakota, Ohio, Pennsylvania,[2] South Carolina, South Dakota, Tennessee, Texas, Virginia, and Washington.	26
Identification is not required to vote beyond the standard established in the Help America Vote Act (identification is required for first-time voters who registered to vote by mail and did not provide verification of their identity).	California, District of Columbia, Idaho, Illinois, Iowa, Maine, Maryland, Massachusetts, Michigan, Minnesota, Mississippi, Nebraska, Nevada, New Hampshire, New Jersey, New York, North Carolina, Oklahoma, Oregon,[3] Rhode Island, Utah, Vermont, West Virginia, Wisconsin, and Wyoming.	25

[1] Identification is required for first-time voters only in Kansas.
[2] Identification is required for first-time voters only in Pennsylvania.
[3] Oregon is a voting by mail state.

Source: League of Women Voters Education Fund. 2009. Voting in Your State. Accessed March 11, 2009, from: http://www.vote411.org/bystate.php; and Project Vote. March 23, 2007. Restrictive Voter Identification Requirements. Accessed March 23, 2009, from: http://projectvote.org/.

by a six to three margin, the lower court rulings were upheld by the High Court.[25] Justice John Paul Stevens wrote the majority opinion. He was joined by Chief Justice John Roberts, and Justices Antonin Scalia, Anthony Kennedy, Clarence Thomas, and Samuel Alito. The dissenters included Justices David Souter, Ruth Bader Ginsburg, and Stephen Breyer.[26]

In his opinion, Justice Stevens reasoned that:

In their briefs, petitioners stress the fact that all of the Republicans in the General Assembly voted in favor of SEA 483 and the Democrats were unanimous in opposing it. In her opinion rejecting petitioners' facial challenge, Judge Barker noted that the litigation was the result of a partisan dispute that had "spilled out of the state house into the courts." It is fair to infer that partisan considerations may have played a significant role in the decision to enact SEA 483. If such considerations had provided the only justification for a photo identification requirement, we may also assume that SEA 483 would suffer the same fate as the poll tax at issue in *Harper*. But if a nondiscriminatory law is supported by valid neutral justifications, those justifications should not be disregarded simply because partisan interests may have provided one motivation for the votes of individual legislators. The state interests identified as justifications for SEA 483 are both neutral and sufficiently strong to require us to reject petitioners' facial attack on the statute. The application of the statute to the vast majority of Indiana voters is amply justified by the valid interest in protecting "the integrity and reliability of the electoral process."[27]

Though Justice Stevens and the others in the majority did note that the statute would place a heavier burden on elderly persons born out-of-state who may have difficulty in obtaining a birth certificate, citizens of limited financial and personal resources, the homeless, as well as people with a religious objection to being photographed, they nevertheless concluded that the burden was sufficiently mitigated by the state's interest in reducing election fraud.[28]

In dissent, Justice David Souter stated emphatically that:

> The upshot is this. Tens of thousands of voting-age residents lack the necessary photo identification. A large proportion of them are likely to be in bad shape economically. The Voter ID Law places hurdles in the way of either getting an ID or of voting provisionally, and they translate into nontrivial economic costs. There is accordingly no reason to doubt that a significant number of state residents will be discouraged or disabled from voting.[29]

To Justice Souter, the most important aspect of Indiana's voter identification law is the justification used by proponents that the law is needed to combat voter fraud. He did not find any substance to this contention, however:

> To begin with, requiring a voter to show photo identification before casting a regular ballot addresses only one form of voter fraud: in-person voter impersonation. The photo ID requirement leaves untouched the problems of absentee-ballot fraud, which (unlike in-person voter impersonation) is a documented problem in Indiana; of registered voters voting more than once in different counties or in different states; of felons and other disqualified individuals voting in their own names; of vote buying, ballot stuffing, ballot miscounting, and/or voter intimidation; or any other type of electoral corruption. And even the State's interest in deterring a voter from showing up at the polls and claiming to be someone he is not must, in turn, be discounted

for the fact that the State has not come across a single instance of in-person impersonation fraud in all of Indiana's history.[30]

Justice Souter determined that Indiana's voter identification law was unconstitutional. To him, state officials failed to justify the limitations placed upon the paramount right to vote, and the law had the effect of imposing an unreasonable and irrelevant burden on voters who happened to be poor and elderly.

FEDERALISM AND POLITICAL CULTURE

A great deal of diversity exists between and among the states, and this has been generally known for some time. Because the United States is a federal republic, power is constitutionally divided between the national government and the state governments. The prominent political scientist, Daniel Elazar, characterized federalism as

> the mode of political organization that unites separate polities within an overarching political system by distributing power among general and constituent governments in a manner designed to protect the existence and authority of both. By requiring that basic policies be made and implemented through a process of negotiation that involves all policies concerned, federal systems enable all to share in the overall system's decision-making and executing processes. In its simplest form, federalism means political integration through the compounding of political systems that continue to exist within the new whole. In a larger sense, however, federalism is more than an arrangement of governmental structures; it is a mode of political activity that requires the extension of certain kinds of cooperative relationships throughout any political system it animates.[31]

The Framers of the U.S. Constitution determined that federal law supersedes state law via Article VI, though they obviously afforded state officials a significant level of latitude in running elections in the United States. The differential approaches taken by state officials all across the country, encompassed in Tables 2.1–2.7, toward elections and voting is largely a reflection of political culture, which, according to Professor Elazar, is "the particular pattern of orientation to political action in which each political system is embedded."[32] Essentially, political culture refers to how different groups of people define politics and the proper role of government in society.

Professor Elazar contends that political culture is rooted in two contrasting conceptions of the American political order, both of which can be traced back to the earliest "settlement" of the nation by Europeans. From one conception, the political order is viewed as a marketplace where the primary relationships are products of bargaining between individual citizens and organized interest groups acting in their own self-interest.[33] This conforms to the Framers' understanding of basic human behavior as documented in James Madison's notes of the Philadelphia Convention.[34] The political order is viewed as a commonwealth in the second conception. In this context, citizens cooperate with one another to create and maintain the best government in order to implement shared moral principles. Throughout American history, these conceptions have rendered a measurable influence on government, politics, and public policy.[35]

Based on these conceptions of American society, the American national culture is a synthesis of three major political subcultures that exist simultaneously and often overlap. Each subculture reflects historical migration patterns that have led certain people of different origins and backgrounds across the United States. The subcultures are as follows: moralistic, individualistic, and traditionalistic. According to the person who crafted these identities:

> The names given the three political subcultures are meant to be descriptive, not evaluative. By the same token, the descriptions of the three that follow are intended to be models or ideal types that are not likely to be fully extant in the real world. Each of the three reflects its own particular synthesis of the marketplace and the commonwealth.[36]

The Moralistic Subculture

To citizens in a moralistic political culture, the commonwealth is emphasized as the basis for democratic government and politics is viewed in a rather favorable manner. Citizens are expected to be active participants in the democratic process in order to advance some collective notion of the greater public good. The role of government is to promote the general welfare of all the people and not simply narrow interests. The moral obligations of those who participate in governance are more demanding than the moral obligations of the marketplace. Politicians and public officials are not expected to financially benefit from political activities.[37] Moralistic subcultures are primarily located in the northern part of the United States, moving westward and southwestward in areas initially settled by the Puritans of New England. The Puritans desired to establish a holy commonwealth, a "good" society.[38]

The Individualistic Subculture

Residents in an individualistic political culture emphasize the conception of democracy as a marketplace. Government exists for utilitarian reasons and should address only those functions that are demanded by the people. Ideological concerns are not very important in an individualistic culture; rather, a businesslike conception of politics that supports the development of professional politicians pervades. There is a rather strong tendency for citizens in this subculture to view politics as a dirty business. Unlike the Puritan roots in the moralistic political culture, ethnic groups from non-Puritan England and the interior Germanic states settled in the mid-Atlantic region and later traveled westward.[39]

The Traditionalistic Subculture

Settlers in the American South were primarily landed gentry who sought individual freedom and economic opportunities in a plantation-centered agricultural system based on slavery.[40] The traditionalistic political culture reflects an older, precommercial perspective that generally accepts hierarchy as a natural order of things in which politicians tend to be elites who seek to maintain their privileged status in society. Those who are at the top of the social and economic structures are expected to take a dominant role in government. Similar to its moralistic counterpart, government is perceived to have a positive role in the community, but instead of emphasizing widespread political participation, a traditionalistic political culture functions to limit political power to relatively small and self-perpetuating groups drawn from an established elite who inherit their right to govern through social status or family connections.[41] Included in Table 2.8 is a comparison of the three subcultures on conceptions of government, politics, and bureaucracy.

According to Professor Elazar, 17 states are classified as having a predominantly moralistic political culture. Another 17 states are identified as having a predominantly individualistic political culture. The remaining 16 states are categorized as having a predominantly traditionalistic political culture.[42] Because the District of Columbia is incorporated in this analysis, it is included in the categorization scheme based primarily on Professor Elazar's classification criteria as well as the geographic location of the District. It is classified as having a predominantly individualistic subculture as such.[43] The states are listed by subculture in Table 2.9.

SUMMARY

The comparison of voting laws in the 50 states and the District of Columbia is not exhaustive but is intended to be illustrative in nature. The state laws are contextual and reflective of their respective histories as well as their political systems. If anything, the discussion in this chapter should enhance the understanding that election law in the United States is highly decentralized, diverse, and complicated by definition.

Table 2.8
Characteristics of the Three Political Subcultures

Concepts	Moralistic	Individualistic	Traditionalistic
Government			
How is government viewed?	Government is viewed as a commonwealth	Government is viewed as a marketplace	Government is viewed as a means of maintaining the existing order
What are the appropriate spheres of government activity?	Any area that will enhance the community though nongovernmental action is preferred; social as well as economic regulation is considered legitimate	Largely economic; economic development is favored	Those that maintain traditional patterns
Should new programs be created?	Will initiate without public pressure if believed to be in public interest	Will only initiate if demanded by public opinion	Will only initiate if program serves the interest of the governing elite
Bureaucracy			
How is the bureaucracy viewed?	Positively	Ambivalently	Negatively
What kind of merit system is favored?	Strong	Loosely implemented	None
Politics (Patterns of Belief)			
How is politics viewed?	Healthy	Dirty	A privilege
Politics (Patterns of Participation)			
Who should participate in politics?	Everyone	Professionals	The appropriate elite
What is the role of political parties?	Vehicles to attain goals believed to be in the public interest	Act as business organizations	Vehicle of reruitment of people to offices not desired by elites
Should political parties be cohesive?	Parties are subordinate to principles and issues	Strong level of cohesion is desirable	Highly personal matter

Concepts	Moralistic	Individualistic	Traditionalistic
Politics (Patterns of Competition)			
How is political competition viewed?	Competition should be about substantive issues	Competition should be between parties and not over issues	Competition should be between elite-dominated factions within a dominant party
What is the orientation toward political competition?	Orientation should be toward winning office for greater opportunity to implement policies and programs	Orientation should be toward winning office for tangible rewards	Orientation is dependent on political values of the elite

Source: Elazar, Daniel J. 1984. *American Federalism: A View from the States* (3rd ed.). New York: Harper & Row, 120–121.

Table 2.9
Political Culture and the American States

Political Culture	States with this Predominant Culture	N
Moralistic	California, Colorado, Idaho, Iowa, Kansas, Maine, Michigan, Minnesota, Montana, New Hampshire, North Dakota, Oregon, South Dakota, Washington, Wisconsin, Utah, and Vermont.	17
Individualistic	Alaska, Connecticut, Delaware, District of Columbia, Hawaii, Illinois, Indiana, Maryland, Massachusetts, Missouri, Nebraska, Nevada, New Jersey, New York, Ohio, Pennsylvania, Rhode Island, and Wyoming.	18
Traditionalistic	Alabama, Arizona, Arkansas, Florida, Georgia, Kentucky, Louisiana, Mississippi, New Mexico, North Carolina, Oklahoma, South Carolina, Tennessee, Texas, Virginia, and West Virginia.	16

Source: Elazar, Daniel J. 1984. *American Federalism: A View from the States* (3rd ed.). New York: Harper & Row, 136.

Chapter 3

VOTER TURNOUT IN THE AMERICAN STATES

Voter turnout is not always measured in the same manner by scholars. This reality also holds true for practitioners and journalists alike. Thus, an essential starting point in any discussion of voter turnout is ascertaining how the concept should be measured before rendering any conclusions and/or policy recommendations.

MEASURING CONCEPTS IN THE SOCIAL SCIENCES

Measurement is a crucial component of evaluation research and design.[1] A diversity of opinions exist in the scholarly community with regard to measurement, as is depicted in the case of school desegregation policy.[2] For a few decades, scholars debated the plausibility of using the Index of Dissimilarity, a racial balance indicator, to accurately measure school desegregation. The Index of Dissimilarity, D, is a statistic, ranging from 0–100, that represents the percentage of African American students who would have to be reassigned to Caucasian schools, if no Caucasians are reassigned, in order to have the same proportion of African Americans in each school as in the district as a whole. A score of zero is indicative of perfect racial balance, meaning that no African American students need to be reassigned and that the racial proportion of students in each school is the same as in the entire district. A score of 100 results in perfect racial imbalance, that is, all of the African American students need to be reassigned, if no Caucasians are reassigned, in order to achieve perfect racial balance. A situation of perfect racial imbalance would be indicative of a dual school system, something that is forbidden under the Supreme Court's decree in *Brown v. Board of Education of Topeka, Kansas*.[3] *D* could be modified to account for changing demographics, such as the influx of Latino Americans into many areas of the country.[4]

Other social scientists tout the relative advantage of measuring segregation by utilizing the Interracial Exposure Index (*Smw*). *Smw* is equal to the proportion of Caucasian students in the average minority child's school. The number of minority students in each school is multiplied by the proportion of Caucasian students in the same school. This number is summed for all schools and divided by the number of minority students in the school system to produce a weighted average—the proportion Caucasian in the average minority child's school. While *D* is a standardized statistic (0–100), *Smw* is an unstandardized mean-based statistic. The lowest score that can be generated is zero, meaning that minority children are not exposed to any nonminority (Caucasian) children. The upper limit depends on the percentage of Caucasians in the school district.[5]

Measures of central tendency (*Smw*) refer to interracial exposure or contact between the races. Measures of dispersion (*D*) examine the differences in the distribution of social groups (e.g., Caucasians and African Americans) in a particular spatial unit (e.g., school districts). Thus, segregation indexes quantify the deviation of a set of schools from a baseline of no segregation. Accordingly, *D* is both a reasonable and functional measure of segregation. The measure captures the phenomenon of interest without making extraneous assumptions. The same does not hold true for *Smw*, however. Interracial exposure indexes are predicated upon an important theoretical assumption: that "white flight" is a common reaction by Caucasians in school desegregation policy. Thus, researchers who utilize *Smw* not only seek to capture the racial mixing of students, but also simultaneously provide an indicator of "white flight."[6] The assumption that Caucasians will "flee" desegregation orders is overly simplistic because decreases in Caucasian enrollments over the past few decades in urban public schools are likely due to a number of factors, including, *inter alia,* social class, and a declining birth rate.[7]

MEASURING VOTER TURNOUT IN A REASONABLE AND FUNCTIONAL MANNER

Not unlike the debate over measuring segregation effectively, contemporary political scientists have largely identified two dominant approaches to measuring voter turnout: voting age population (VAP) and voting eligible population (VEP). Bear in mind the crucial importance of utilizing an indicator that actually measures the phenomenon of interest without the inclusion of theoretical assumptions that may, in fact, be largely dubious.

Voting Age Population

The traditional measure of voter turnout in the United States is a simple fraction. It is the percentage of the voting age population that actually voted in an election. Since 1972, this has entailed all Americans 18 and older. Prior to the 1972 elections, it meant all those 21 and older who voted.[8] The numerator is the total number of voters, and the denominator is the voting age population:

Voter Turnout = Total number of voters / Total Voting Age Population (VAP)

As Professor Walter Dean Burnham has explained:

> There are two points of attack: the numerator and the denominator from which that ratio we call a turnout estimate is derived. We turn first to the numerator, the report of votes cast in various sources. The conduct of elections and the reporting of the results in the United States has been almost exclusively the task of the individual states.[9]

As Professor Burnham notes, historically, two problems have arisen with regard to the integrity of the numerator:

> The first of these is that particular form of election fraud which involves corrupt surplusage or ballot-box stuffing. The second major problem arises from errors (presumably honest) of count or tabulation.[10]

Many historians believe that claims of universal ballot-box stuffing were undoubtedly exaggerated, particularly in the 19th century. Even though some incidents did occur, election fraud greatly curtailed when the administration of elections was markedly altered when personal registration statutes were passed and implemented across the states.[11] Human errors can generally occur in one of two places. They can occur in the primary source itself (local returns) and/or at the state level as well.[12]

In terms of the denominator, Professor Burnham reported about 25 years ago that:

> A direct challenge is launched against the underlying accuracy of the state and national turnout estimates published in the 1975 edition of *Historical Abstract of the United States*. We hope that we have demonstrated that, in the main, the figures of votes cast published in *Presidential Ballots* and other sources are accurate, differ trivially from each other, and usually (though not always) represent an honest count by local election officials. To the extent that this is so, whatever is left of the argument that the turnout estimates are *grossly* inaccurate, granted the shape of the underlying data on which they rest, must be found in the estimates of the potential electorate.[13]

An extensive scrutiny of the estimates of the voting age population[14] led Burnham to conclude that broad or systematic error, never mind rampant fraudulent voting, does not occur and that the estimates of the voting age population historically are reliable so long as sufficient detail is afforded to the creation of accurate decision rules to ensure that the concept measured is depicted in an intuitive and reasonable manner.[15] This conclusion with regard to the denominator (voting age population) was also offered by another prominent political scientist:

> The voting-age population is the standard base (denominator) for estimating turnout rates in the United States. This is both because the voting-age population is a good approximation of the actual number of eligible voters and because adjusting the voting-age population to remove legally ineligible voters (that is, aliens) is a difficult and imprecise process. Furthermore—though this is little known—citizenship is not a constitutional requirement for voting in the United States. Both the time it takes to become a citizen (national) and the actual restriction of suffrage to citizens (state) are matters of legislation. Thus at the most basic level of the system, the voting-age population *is* the eligible population. For all these reasons the term "turnout" in this book generally refers to turnout of the voting-age population.[16]

A more recent trend on the part of some researchers has resulted in the utilization of a different denominator: voting eligible population.

Voting Eligible Population

Professor Michael P. McDonald utilizes voting eligible population as the denominator at the present time on the United States Elections Project Web site.[17] He asserts that:

> Voter turnout rates presented here show that the much-lamented decline in voter participation is an artifact of poor measurement. Previously, turnout rates were calculated by dividing the number of votes by what is called the "voting-age population" which consists of everyone 18 and older residing in the United States. This includes persons ineligible to vote, mainly non-citizens and ineligible felons, and excludes overseas eligible voters. When turnout rates are calculated for those eligible to vote, a new picture of turnout emerges, which exhibits no decline since 1972. Indeed, turnout rates appear to have been restored to their earlier high levels as of 2008.[18]

The same researcher, in an earlier work, touts the accuracy of utilizing the voting eligible population as the denominator:

Our more accurate VEP uses a variety of government statistical series to adjust the VAP. We remove noncitizens using estimates found in the Current Population Survey (CPS) and the full Census of Population. We remove persons who are ineligible due to criminality based on Department of Justice statistics on the correctional population. We add military and civilian personnel living overseas using statistics from the Bureau of the Census, Department of Defense, Office of Personnel Management, and the United States Consular Service.[19]

The use of the voting eligible population denominator results in the conclusion that the apparent decline in voter participation in American national elections since 1972 is an illusion and not reflective of reality. Contrary to the belief that American voters are "disappearing,"[20] others note that "[w]e show that although the turnout rate outside the South is lower than in the 1950s and early 1960s, there has been no downward trend during the last 30 years. The apparent decline since 1972 is an artifact of using the voting-age population (VAP) to calculate the turnout rate."[21] Thus, the use of two different denominators, VAP and VEP, prompts researchers to promulgate very different conclusions. Those utilizing VAP in their research maintain that voter turnout in the United States has been declining steadily since it peaked in the 1960s.[22] Political scientists who incorporate VEP in their evaluations concede that voter turnout in the United States has declined slightly since the 1960s but that it is rather inconsequential in nature and likely the result of institutional factors.[23]

One Best Measure

Following the 1996 elections, an interesting debate regarding the measurement of voter turnout was presented in *The Public Perspective*. One scholar,[24] Professor Peter Bruce, was very critical of the turnout data promulgated by officials at the Committee for the Study of the American Electorate (CSAE):

Two days after the 1996 elections, the media proclaimed that more eligible voters had abstained than had voted, that turnout had fallen to 48.8%—its lowest level since 1924—and that state turnouts had hit such abysmal lows as 44% in New York and 39% in California. This depiction has been widely accepted. But despite its acceptance, it's wrong. Voter turnout equals the total number of votes cast divided by the eligible electorate. The "experts" erred regarding both numerator and denominator by: (1) calculating turnout with incomplete returns, and (2) equating the U.S. Census Bureau's voting age population (VAP) figures with the eligible electorate, even though the VAP is inflated by almost 10% with people legally ineligible to vote. Both missteps led to the exaggerating and sensationalizing turnout decline. If turnout is calculated with complete returns and with the VAP purged of ineligibles, we see that a clear majority—54.5%—of eligible voters cast ballots, with 53.7% voting for president. These figures exceed 1988's turnout rate of 52.2%, and thus was not the lowest turnout rate since 1924.[25]

Professor Bruce's criticism is particularly poignant of scholars who use VAP as the denominator in the measurement of voter turnout:

> Inaccurate statistics on turnout confuse intellectual discourse. They also do injustice to activists, government officials, and the public by depriving them of information needed to accurately assess the effects of their reforms, get-out-the-vote drives, and voting efforts, especially when the actual turnouts are better than reported. By systematically underestimating turnouts, the experts may contribute to the very voting decline they bemoan, by purveying an image of American politics as more moribund than it is.[26]

Professor Curtis Gans of the CSAE provided a strong rejoinder to these conclusions. Professor Bruce was critical of both the numerator and denominator used by the CSAE researchers, though he was particularly at odds with the denominator. According to Professor Gans, Professor Bruce preferred to utilize the total number of ballots cast (as opposed to those who voted for president) as the numerator, but this information was available in only 36 states in 1996 and fewer states than that in the past. Thus, the presidential vote provided for a consistent manner to analyze voter turnout over time.[27]

With regard to the denominator, Mr. Gans contends that Mr. Bruce ignored three factors in his critique of the denominator used by the CSAE: naturalization (more immigrants were becoming naturalized), age-eligible citizens living abroad (a reasonable estimate of this subgroup was provided by the U.S. Defense Department, the Bureau of Consular Affairs, and the Office of Personnel Management), and the Census undercount (the Census's VAP estimates are based on interpolation from the decennial census, which typically undercounts the population but not to the same extent as those researchers relying upon the VEP).[28]

Professor Gans' criticism of Professor Bruce is summarized in the following passage:

> Foolish consistency may be the hobgoblin of small minds. But consistency and comparability are the only way that students and scholars of voting behavior can do longitudinal research. I know of no serious scholar in the field of election data who does not strive for such consistency (with admittedly inadequate figures) to provide historical perspective. They (we) do not compare turnout in mid-term elections with turnout in presidential elections

(except to note similar trends). And they (we) seek to find a common basis for understanding what has been happening in American politics, which can only be seen over time and through the prism of a consistent set of figures.[29]

Professor Gans has made a compelling substantive argument in defense of the plausibility of using VAP as the denominator when measuring voter turnout. Data are estimates of reality that assist scholars in gaining a better understanding of their universe over time; the knowledge in question in turn can be shared with the general public in the pursuit of a more enlightened understanding of the past, present, and future.

At the present time, in presidential election years, the numerator is the vote for president, even though this number is typically about 1 percent lower than the actual number of citizens who go to the polls. It is somewhat lower because some state officials do not keep records of all those who go to the polls. In midterm elections, the numerator is the total number of votes for the statewide race in each state that draws the highest number of votes. In those states that do not have statewide races, the numerator is the aggregate total of votes for the U.S. House of Representatives. This total tends to be between 1 and 1.5 percent lower than the actual vote.[30]

According to Professor Gans, voter turnout is not the percentage of those registered who voted for basically three reasons:

1. Using voter registration as a denominator does not account for the whole electorate, including those who are not registered to vote. This figure inflates voter turnout accordingly.

2. Changes in voter registration laws can have a significant affect on voter turnout. While voter registration levels have increased after Congress allowed for national mail registration, registration at motor vehicle bureaus, and social service agencies, voter turnout does not necessarily increase as a result.

3. Registration figures are subject to the fluctuations of election administration. By way of illustration, when state officials conduct a thorough purge of registration lists close to an election, its registration figures will be lower and thus its percentage of registered voting will be higher.[31]

With regard to the most contentious aspect of measuring voter turnout (the denominator), the utilization of a modified version of VAP is the optimum manner in which to calculate voter turnout. For many years, this meant using the Census Bureau's estimates of the November age-eligible population (VAP) to determine turnout. Yet, in recent years, this figure was legitimately criticized because it included noncitizens in particular.[32] But Professor Burnham has been producing a denominator of age-eligible citizens (age-eligible population minus age-eligible noncitizens) by inter-polating data between each decennial census. In spite of a different per-spective on the matter that is touted by Professor McDonald, this is the best estimate of voter turnout currently available due to two primary factors.[33]

First, voter turnout statistics are not simply short-term phenomena. These data must provide a historical comparison with previous years. The data needed to address some of the shortcomings of VAP are simply not available or are not reliable over time.[34] Second, the most important short-coming of VAP, according to CSAE officials, entails noncitizens. Professor Burnham's reform of VAP data that allows researchers to factor out non-citizens has had the cumulative effect of ensuring the use of VAP as the denominator in the provision of a voter turnout figure that is an accurate depiction of human behavior and one that can be used for comparative purposes over time.[35]

A Final Word on Measuring Voter Turnout

Structural rules are important in American politics. This reality can-not be simply ignored for issues of convenience. Many contend that state registration laws affect voter turnout, and this issue will be revisited later. In addition, the fact that most state laws prohibit convicted felons from vot-ing, some for extended periods of time, including their entire lives, impacts voter turnout. It is not incumbent upon the comparative evaluator to make allowances for this policy when comparing voter turnout in the United States or comparing U.S. voter turnout internationally. Using VEP as the denominator is implausible precisely because structural rules and human decision-making processes are issues of direct salience to voting. Units of analysis should be analyzed in an equitable manner by the social scientist so that bias is minimized and citizens can make their own judgments based upon a concrete and substantive presentation of the status quo.

NATIONAL VOTER TURNOUT IN U.S. PRESIDENTIAL ELECTIONS

Voter turnout (the percentage of the voting age population that voted) has fluctuated over the last eight decades. In general, however, it has declined over time with some exceptions. The turnout data for U.S. presidential elections between 1932 and 2008 are available in Table 3.1. Turnout is pre-sented from the highest level (1960) through the lowest rate (1996) during this time period in Table 3.2.

Turnout in four elections in the 1960s and 1950s (1960, 1952, 1964, and 1968) exceeded 60 percent, with the highest turnout garnered in the John Kennedy versus Richard Nixon contest in 1960. When 18, 19, and 20 year

Table 3.1
Voter Turnout in U.S. Presidential Elections, 1932–2008 (Percentage of Voting Age Population that Voted)

Presidential Election	Voter Turnout
1932	52.6
1936	56.9
1940	58.8
1944	56.1
1948	51.1
1952	61.6
1956	59.3
1960	62.8
1964	61.4
1968	60.7
1972	55.1
1976	53.6
1980	52.8
1984	53.3
1988	50.3
1992	55.2
1996	49.0
2000	50.3
2004	55.6
2008	56.8

Sources: U.S. Census Bureau. 2009. *The 2009 Statistical Abstract*. Elections: Voting-Age Population and Voter Participation. Accessed August 10, 2009, from: http://www.census.gov/compendia/statab/tables/09s0402.pdf (1932–2004); and U.S. Elections Project. 2009. Voter Turnout. Accessed May 21, 2009, from: http://elections.gmu.edu/voter_turnout.htm.

olds were included in the voting age population in 1972, turnout declined by over 5 percent. It has never been over the 60 percent threshold since the Twenty-Sixth Amendment was added to the Constitution.

The average voter turnout during these 20 presidential elections is 55.7 percent. Yet with the inclusion of more youthful voters beginning in 1972, turnout has only been higher than the average for the 1932–2008 time period once, and that was the 2008 presidential contest between Barack Obama and John McCain. Voter participation in this historic election was the highest since 1968, though not as high as many analysts were projecting on the eve of the election. Voter turnout has only dipped below half of

Table 3.2
Rank Order of Voter Turnout in U.S. Presidential Elections, 1932–2008
(Percentage of Voting Age Population that Voted)

Voter Turnout	Presidential Election	Democratic Candidate	Republican Candidate
1. 62.8	1960	John Kennedy	Richard Nixon
2. 61.6	1952	Adlai Stevenson	Dwight Eisenhower
3. 61.4	1964	Lyndon Johnson	Barry Goldwater
4. 60.7	1968	Hubert Humphrey	Richard Nixon
5. 59.3	1956	Adlai Stevenson	Dwight Eisenhower
6. 58.8	1940	Franklin Roosevelt	Wendell Willkie
7. 56.9	1936	Franklin Roosevelt	Alfred Landon
8. 56.8	2008	Barack Obama	John McCain
9. 56.1	1944	Franklin Roosevelt	Thomas Dewey
10. 55.6	2004	John Kerry	George W. Bush
11. 55.2	1992	Bill Clinton	George H.W. Bush
12. 55.1	1972	George McGovern	Richard Nixon
13. 53.6	1976	Jimmy Carter	Gerald Ford
14. 53.3	1984	Walter Mondale	Ronald Reagan
15. 52.8	1980	Jimmy Carter	Ronald Reagan
16. 52.6	1932	Franklin Roosevelt	Herbert Hoover
17. 51.1	1948	Harry Truman	Thomas Dewey
18. 50.3	1988	Michael Dukakis	George H.W. Bush
18. 50.3	2000	Al Gore	George W. Bush
20. 49.0	1996	Bill Clinton	Robert Dole

Sources: U.S. Census Bureau. 2009. *The 2009 Statistical Abstract*. Elections: Voting-Age Population and Voter Participation. Accessed August 10, 2009, from: http://www.census.gov/compendia/statab/tables/09s0402.pdf (1932–2004); and U.S. Elections Project. 2009. Voter Turnout. Accessed May 21, 2009, from: http://elections.gmu.edu/voter_turnout.htm.

the voting age population once since 1932, and this occurred in the 1996 election between Bill Clinton and Robert Dole.

The diversity between and among the states with regard to voter turnout is depicted in Table 3.3, which includes a rank ordering of the states in the 2008 presidential election. Minnesota had the highest voter turnout of any state (73.2%), while Hawaii had the lowest (45.1%). This is over a 28 percent difference between number 1 and 51 (the District of Columbia is included in the analysis).[36] From one election to the next, there is generally a good deal of consistency with regard to voter turnout

Table 3.3
Voter Turnout in the States, 2008 Presidential Election (Percentage of Voting Age Population that Voted)

State	Voter Turnout
1. Minnesota	73.2
2. Maine	70.1
3. New Hampshire	69.4
4. Wisconsin	69.0
5. Iowa	67.0
6. Vermont	65.9
7. Michigan	65.7
8. Montana	65.6
9. Missouri	65.0
10. Ohio	65.0
11. Alaska	64.2
12. Colorado	64.0
13. North Dakota	63.5
14. South Dakota	62.8
15. Wyoming	62.7
16. Virginia	62.4
17. Oregon	62.3
18. Pennsylvania	62.0
19. Delaware	61.6
20. North Carolina	61.4
21. Connecticut	61.2
22. Maryland	61.1
23. Massachusetts	60.5
24. Washington	60.3
25. Nebraska	59.8
26. Mississippi	59.2
27. Alabama	59.1
28. Louisiana	58.8
29. Idaho	58.6
29. Kansas	58.6
31. Florida	58.4
32. New Jersey	58.3
33. Indiana	57.3
34. Rhode Island	57.2
35. Illinois	56.7

(continued)

Table 3.3

Voter Turnout in the States, 2008 Presidential Election (Percentage of Voting Age Population that Voted) *(continued)*

State	Voter Turnout
36. Kentucky	55.9
36. New Mexico	55.9
36. South Carolina	55.9
39. District of Columbia	55.2
40. Georgia	54.7
40. Tennessee	54.7
42. Oklahoma	53.3
43. Arkansas	50.3
44. New York	50.1
45. Utah	50.0
46. Nevada	49.9
46. West Virginia	49.9
48. California	49.4
49. Arizona	47.4
50. Texas	45.6
51. Hawaii	45.1

Source: U.S. Census Bureau. 2009. *The 2009 Statistical Abstract*. Elections: Voting-Age Population and Voter Participation. Accessed August 10, 2009, from: http://www.census.gov/compendia/statab/tables/09s0402.pdf; and U.S. Elections Project. 2009. Voter Turnout. Accessed May 21, 2009, from: http://elections.gmu.edu/voter_turnout.htm.

in the states. For example, when comparing the 2000 and 2008 presidential elections, 7 states were in the top 10 in voter turnout in both elections: Minnesota, Maine, New Hampshire, Wisconsin, Iowa, Vermont, and Montana, where Minnesota, Maine, and Wisconsin were first, second, and fourth, respectively, in both elections. Conversely, 7 states were in the bottom 10 in voter turnout in both elections as well: Arkansas, Nevada, West Virginia, California, Arizona, Texas, and Hawaii. Hawaii registered the lowest voter turnout in both the 2000 and 2008 elections.[37]

NATIONAL VOTER TURNOUT IN U.S. MIDTERM ELECTIONS

Voter turnout data for U.S. midterm (nonpresidential) elections are available from 1934–2006 in Table 3.4. Turnout is presented from the highest

Table 3.4
Voter Turnout in U.S. Midterm Elections, 1934–2006 (Percentage of Voting Age Population that Voted)

Midterm Election	Voter Turnout
1934	42.1
1938	Not available
1942	32.5
1946	37.1
1950	41.2
1954	41.7
1958	43.0
1962	45.4
1966	45.4
1970	43.6
1974	35.7
1978	34.5
1982	37.7
1986	33.6
1990	33.6
1994	36.5
1998	33.1
2002	34.7
2006	35.8

Source: U.S. Census Bureau. 2009. *The 2009 Statistical Abstract*. Elections: Voting-Age Population and Voter Participation. Accessed August 10, 2009, from: http://www.census.gov/compendia/statab/tables/09s0402.pdf.

level (1962 and 1966) through the lowest rate (1942 during World War II) during this time period in Table 3.5.

Turnout in seven elections (1962, 1966, 1970, 1958, 1934, 1954, and 1950) exceeded 40 percent; otherwise turnout in U.S. midterm elections, particularly since 1974, has been in the 30th percentile. It has never been over the 40 percent threshold since the Twenty-Sixth Amendment was added to the Constitution.

The average voter turnout during these 18 midterm elections is 38.2 percent. Yet with the inclusion of more youthful voters beginning in the 1974 midterm election, turnout has been consistently below this average, peaking at a high of 37.7 percent during President Ronald Reagan's first midterm election in 1982.

Table 3.5
**Rank Order of Voter Turnout in U.S. Midterm Elections, 1934–2006
(Percentage of Voting Age Population that Voted)**

Voter Turnout	Midterm Election[1]
1. 45.4	1962
1. 45.4	1966
3. 43.6	1970
4. 43.0	1958
5. 42.1	1934
6. 41.7	1954
7. 41.2	1950
8. 37.7	1982
9. 37.1	1946
10. 36.5	1994
11. 35.8	2006
12. 35.7	1974
13. 34.7	2002
14. 34.5	1978
15. 33.6	1986
15. 33.6	1990
17. 33.1	1998
18. 32.5	1942

[1] Note that data for the 1938 elections are not available.

Source: U.S. Census Bureau. 2009. *The 2009 Statistical Abstract*. Elections: Voting-Age Population and Voter Participation. Accessed August 10, 2009, from: http://www.census.gov/compendia/statab/tables/09s0402.pdf.

VOTER TURNOUT IN THE FREE WORLD

According to officials at the Freedom House, an independent nongovernmental organization, there are 89 free countries and 62 partly free countries, and 42 countries are classified as not free.[38] The *Freedom in the World* survey provides an annual evaluation of the progress and decline of freedom in 193 nations in the world. Two broad categories are encompassed in the survey: political rights and civil liberties. Each country is assigned a rating for each category based on a seven-point ordinal scale (1 represents the most free, while 7 is indicative of the least free).[39] Free countries are those whose ratings average between 1 and 2.5;[40] partly free countries average between 3 and 5;[41] and not free countries average between 5.5 and 7 on this scale.[42]

In order to compare voter turnout in the United States with other democracies in the world, all free countries will be utilized by way of illustration. Obviously, there is a significant amount of diversity between and among the nations in this category. Some of the nations are advanced industrialized societies with substantial economic and/or military sectors; others are very small and are not economic or military powers in global politics. In addition, it must be understood that countries vary in terms of frequency of elections, type of election (presidential and/or parliamentary), and whether or not reliable data banks are maintained over longitudinal periods of time. Fortunately, there is a compendium of voter turnout data that is regularly updated for all countries in the world.

The International Institute for Democracy and Electoral Assistance (International IDEA), an intergovernmental organization headquartered in Stockholm, Sweden, provides voter turnout statistics for national presidential and parliamentary elections since 1945.[43] Voter turnout data for all free nations in the world[44] are provided in Table 3.6 using the percentage of the voting age population (VAP) that voted. The most recent year of reliable data is utilized for each country, and the type of election is noted as well.

Given the diversity in this universe of nations along different spectrums, it would be undoubtedly implausible to rank order the free countries of the world in terms of voter turnout. Yet even the most casual analyst cannot help but notice that the vast majority of all free nations routinely have higher voter turnout rates than the United States and, in many cases, by substantial margins. Why is it that so few Americans participate in the electoral process in proportion to citizens in other free societies? Is relatively low voter turnout a troublesome, and even disturbing, pattern of citizen behavior in the world's oldest democracy? In order to address these questions in an enlightened manner, it is essential to engage in a historical investigation of what the Framers created in Philadelphia in 1787. The federal republic that they created and many of the structural rules that were adopted at that time still have a profound effect on the electoral realities of the early 21st century.

SUMMARY

Structural rules governing elections vary widely among the states in America as well as the free nations of the world. Yet by using the percentage of the voting age population that voted as a standard measure of voter turnout, a

Table 3.6
Voter Turnout in the Free World (Percentage of Voting Age Population that Voted)

Nation	Year	Election Type[1]	Voter Turnout
Andorra	2005	PA	20.9
Antigua and Barbuda	2004	PA	76.3
Argentina	2007	PA	70.9
	2007	PR	72.2
Australia	2007	PA	82.7
Austria	2008	PA	75.6
	2004	PR	66.5
Bahamas	2007	PA	69.2
Barbados	1999	PA	68.6
Belgium	2007	PA	86.0
Belize	2008	PA	73.9
Benin	2007	PA	61.8
	2006	PR	82.6
Botswana	2004	PA	44.0
Brazil	2006	PA	83.5
	2006	PR	83.6
Bulgaria	2005	PA	62.4
	2006	PR	46.1
Canada	2008	PA	53.6
Cape Verde	2006	PA	80.0
	2006	PR	78.6
Chile	2005	PA	66.5
	2006	PR	63.0
Costa Rica	2006	PA	54.0
	2006	PR	64.0
Croatia	2007	PA	70.8
	2005	PR	63.4
Cyprus	2006	PA	77.8
	2008	PR	78.8
Czech Republic	2006	PA	65.1
Denmark	2007	PA	83.2
Dominica	2005	PA	82.1
Dominican Republic	2006	PA	56.4
	2008	PR	71.6

Nation	Year	Election Type[1]	Voter Turnout
El Salvador	2006	PA	52.7
	2004	PR	63.1
Estonia	2007	PA	53.4
Finland	2007	PA	68.2
	2006	PR	77.6
France	2007	PA	54.5
	2007	PR	76.8
Germany	2005	PA	72.0
Ghana	2004	PA	80.0
	2004	PR	80.0
Greece	2007	PA	89.0
Grenada	2003	PA	98.2
Guyana	2006	PA	66.4
Hungary	2006	PA	41.1
Iceland	2007	PA	84.6
	2004	PR	63.7
India	2004	PA	60.6
Indonesia	2004	PA	87.6
	2004	PR	74.8
Ireland	2007	PA	68.9
	1997	PR	47.7
Israel	2006	PA	71.2
Italy	2008	PA	79.1
Jamaica	2007	PA	49.6
Japan	2005	PA	66.6
Kiribati	2007	PA	42.5
Latvia	2006	PA	50.2
Lesotho	2007	PA	38.6
Liechtenstein	2005	PA	57.6
Lithuania	2008	PA	46.1
	2004	PR	50.3
Luxembourg	2004	PA	56.5
Mali	2007	PA	39.0
	2007	PR	48.2
Malta	2008	PA	98.4
Marshall Islands	2007	PA	54.6

(continued)

Table 3.6
Voter Turnout in the Free World (Percentage of Voting Age Population that Voted) *(continued)*

Nation	Year	Election Type[1]	Voter Turnout
Mauritius	2000	PA	79.6
Mexico	2006	PA	63.6
	2006	PR	63.3
Micronesia	2007	PA	82.4
Monaco	2008	PA	18.3
Mongolia	2008	PA	60.5
	2005	PR	53.7
Namibia	2004	PA	80.2
	2004	PR	80.9
Nauru	2008	PA	60.6
Netherlands	2006	PA	77.5
New Zealand	2008	PA	77.8
Norway	2005	PA	76.5
Palau	2008	PA	42.6
	2008	PR	67.6
Panama	2004	PA	79.7
	2004	PR	80.3
Peru	2006	PA	84.1
	2006	PR	83.2
Poland	2007	PA	54.2
	2005	PR	51.5
Portugal	2005	PA	69.2
	2006	PR	67.0
Romania	2004	PA	62.3
	2004	PR	58.3
Saint Kitts and Nevis	2004	PA	91.4
Saint Lucia	2006	PA	74.4
Saint Vincent and The Grenadines	2005	PA	58.8
Samoa	2001	PA	76.6
San Marino	2006	PA	98.1
Sao Tome and Principe	2006	PA	62.9
	2006	PR	69.8

Nation	Year	Election Type[1]	Voter Turnout
Serbia	2008	PA	70.2
	2008	PR	69.8
Slovakia	2006	PA	56.4
	2004	PR	44.1
Slovenia	2008	PA	65.0
	2007	PR	61.3
South Africa	2004	PA	56.8
South Korea	2008	PA	46.6
	2007	PR	64.2
Spain	2008	PA	77.9
Suriname	2005	PA	53.0
Sweden	2006	PA	80.6
Switzerland	2007	PA	39.8
Taiwan	2008	PA	56.8
	2008	PR	74.7
Trinidad and Tobago	2007	PA	72.5
Tuvalu	2002	PA	63.1
Ukraine	2007	PA	62.7
	2004	PR	78.1
United Kingdom	2005	PA	58.3
United States	2006	PA	37.3
	2008	PR	58.3
Uruguay	2004	PA	93.1
	2004	PR	91.8
Vanuatu	2008	PA	82.8

[1] Election Type (PA = parliamentary; PR = presidential).

Source: International Institute for Democracy and Electoral Assistance (International IDEA). 2009. Voter Turnout. Accessed August 25, 2009, from: http://www.idea.int/vt/.

great deal of knowledge can be garnered concerning citizen participation in elections. The knowledge in question is fundamental to the reformer who believes that there is room for improvement in any human endeavor, particularly those pertaining to the sovereign citizenry and the representatives who are elected to serve on behalf of the people.

Chapter 4

THE ELECTORAL COLLEGE
AND THE FRAMERS
IN PHILADELPHIA

While the Framers of the Constitution allowed states to essentially run their own elections, Congress intervened in the mid-19th century because of perceptions of voter fraud in presidential elections by requiring that electors be selected on the "Tuesday next after the first Monday in the month of November of the year in which they are appointed."[1] Thus, the presidential election in 1848 was the first one in which Americans in every state voted on the same day.[2] Yet as indicated in Chapter 2, many state laws still generally govern the administration of elections today.[3]

But one of the key structural rules governing elections established by the Framers that is still prevailing law today is the creation of the Electoral College. In lieu of direct election of the president or congressional selection, the Framers devised a mechanism for presidential selection that has resulted in some candidates becoming president even though they lost the popular vote.[4]

ARTICLE II OF THE U.S. CONSTITUTION

The final version of the U.S. Constitution stipulates that a majority of electors has the authority to select a president for a term of four years. Under the original Constitution, there were no term limits for the president.[5] The Framers determined that:

> Each state shall appoint, in such manner as the Legislature thereof may direct, a number of electors, equal to the whole number of Senators and

Representatives to which the State may be entitled in the Congress: but no Senator or Representative, or person holding an office of trust or profit under the United States, shall be appointed an elector.

The electors shall meet in their respective states, and vote by ballot for two persons, of whom one at least shall not be an inhabitant of the same state with themselves. And they shall make a list of all persons voted for, and of the number of votes for each; which list they shall sign and certify, and transmit sealed to the seat of the government of the United States, directed to the President of the Senate. The President of the Senate shall, in the presence of the Senate and House of Representatives, open all the certificates, and the votes shall then be counted. The person having the greatest number of votes shall be the President, if such number be a majority of the whole number of electors appointed; and if there be more than one who have such a majority, and have an equal number of votes, then the House of Representatives shall immediately choose by ballot one of them for President; and if no person have a majority, then from the five highest on the list the said House shall in like manner choose the President. But in choosing the President, the votes shall be taken by States, the representation from each state having one vote; A quorum for a majority of all the states shall be necessary to a choice. In every case, after the choice of a President, the person having the greatest number of votes of the electors shall be the Vice President. But if there should remain two or more who have equal votes, the Senate shall choose from them by ballot the Vice President.

Yet, problems developed with this part of the Constitution in the early years of the republic. The Framers did not envision the evolution of political parties, but in 1796 the system effectively yielded a president from one party (John Adams, Federalist) and a vice president (Thomas Jefferson, Democratic-Republican) of another party. In the following 1800 presidential election, two candidates from the same political party, Vice president Jefferson and Aaron Burr, received the same number of electoral votes, which compelled the House of Representatives to determine the outcome of the election.[6] The emergence of political parties caused failure in the original constitutional design for presidential selection. Subsequently, the Twelfth Amendment was added to the Constitution when it was ratified in 1804.

THE TWELFTH AMENDMENT

The Twelfth Amendment provided several important provisions that were designed to mitigate the political controversies that occurred during the 1796 and 1800 elections:

The electors shall meet in their respective states and vote by ballot for President and Vice-President, one of whom, at least, shall not be an inhabitant of the same state with themselves; they shall name in their ballots the person voted for as President, and in distinct ballots the person voted for as Vice-President, and they shall make distinct lists of all persons voted for as President, and of all persons voted for as Vice-President, and of the number of votes for each, which lists they shall sign and certify, and transmit sealed to the seat of the government of the United States, directed to the President of the Senate; the President of the Senate shall, in the presence of the Senate and House of Representatives, open all the certificates and the votes shall then be counted; the person having the greatest number of votes for President, shall be the President, if such number be a majority of the whole number of electors appointed; and if no person have such majority, then from the persons having the highest numbers not exceeding three on the list of those voted for as President, the House of Representatives shall choose immediately, by ballot, the President. But in choosing the President, the votes shall be taken by states, the representation from each state having one vote; a quorum for this purpose shall consist of a member or members from two-thirds of the states, and a majority of all the states shall be necessary to a choice. And if the House of Representatives shall not choose a President whenever the right of choice shall devolve upon them, before the fourth day of March next following, then the Vice-President shall act as President, as in the case of the death or other constitutional disability of the President. The person having the greatest number of votes as Vice-President, shall be the Vice-President, if such number be a majority of the whole number of electors appointed, and if no person have a majority, then from the two highest numbers on the list, the Senate shall choose the Vice-President; a quorum for the purpose shall consist of two-thirds of the whole number of Senators, and a majority of the whole number shall be necessary to a choice. But no person constitutionally ineligible to the office of President shall be eligible to that of Vice-President of the United States.

Thus, the Twelfth Amendment, for the first time, provided for separate ballots for president and vice president. In addition, vice presidential candidates had to meet the same constitutional requirements as presidential candidates. In cases where no presidential candidate receives a simple majority of the Electoral College vote, the members of the House of Representatives by state delegations (each state has one vote) choose from the top three vote recipients; if a vice presidential candidate does not garner a simple majority of the electors, then she/he is selected by the members of the U.S. Senate.

THE DEBATE ABOUT PRESIDENTIAL SELECTION AT THE PHILADELPHIA CONVENTION

Before engaging in a review of the Framers' debate about presidential selection, it is important to emphasize some fundamental rules that were established before the legislative proceedings commenced in Philadelphia.

First, to reinforce a point made earlier, the Framers decided that none of their deliberations would be shared with reporters. There was a complete news blackout. The windows were closed during the summer months, and sentries were posted outside the Pennsylvania State House so that none of the debates could be overheard by the public. Adherence to this rule was absolutely strict.[7]

A second rule that is paramount in understanding the Framers' debates is that they discussed and debated issues as a Committee of the Whole. In so doing, this allowed the Framers to reconsider every decision that they made. This meant that they discussed and voted on the same issue on many occasions. Most of the work of legislative bodies is done in committees.[8] It is incumbent upon members of a committee to make recommendations to its larger body; in this case, the Framers could reconsider issues if they so desired by rendering the decisions by the Committee of the Whole as recommendations to be reviewed again when the committee turned itself back into the Convention again. It also allowed the delegates who initially lost on substantive matters to try to make their cases again at a later date.[9]

Another point bears reiterating at this juncture. James Madison, who attended every day that the Convention was in session, took detailed notes of the debates that took place. For several decades thereafter, he "corrected" his notes when other records about the Philadelphia Convention became available. To historians, obviously, such an enterprise can be very disconcerting, especially given the fact that none of the other Framers could refute his work because Mr. Madison was the last survivor of those who participated in the Philadelphia Convention. Yet his account is still regarded as the best record of that summer where secrecy was omnipresent. His colleagues in Philadelphia knew that he was keeping an unofficial official record and evidently trusted his discretion, judgment, and sense of fairness.[10]

The Origin of the Debate: The Virginia Plan

The Virginia Plan was presented to the delegates in attendance on Tuesday, May 29, 1787.[11] It was proposed by Edmund Randolph of Virginia. While obviously containing multiple resolutions,[12] as it pertained to presidential selection, Mr. Randolph suggested that:

> Resd. that a National Executive be instituted; to be chosen by the National Legislature for the term of _____ years, to received punctually at stated times, a fixed compensation for the services rendered, in which no increase or diminution shall be made so as to affect the Magistracy, existing at the time of increase or diminution, and to be ineligible a second time; and that besides a general authority to execute the National laws, it ought to enjoy the Executive rights vested in Congress by the Confederation.[13]

No vote was taken on this day as the resolutions comprising the Virginia Plan became a central focus in the multifaceted debates that ensued in Philadelphia.

June 2, 1787

Just a few days after the introduction of the Virginia Plan, two votes were taken on the issue of presidential selection on Saturday, June 2, 1787. James Wilson of Pennsylvania moved the following resolution:

> Resolved that the Executive Magistracy shall be elected in manner following. That the States be divided into _____ Districts—and that the persons, qualified to vote in each District, elect _____ Members for their respective Districts to be electors of the Executive Magistracy. That the electors of the Executive Magistracy meet and they or any _____ of them shall elect by ballot, but not out of their own Body, _____ Person in whom the Executive authority of the national government be vested.[14]

The motion failed. Two state delegations (Pennsylvania and Maryland) voted in favor of it; seven delegations (Massachusetts, Connecticut, Delaware, Virginia, North Carolina, South Carolina, and Georgia) opposed it; and one was divided (New York)[15]

It was then moved to adopt a resolution submitted by Virginia's Edmund Randolph. Regarding the chief executive, the Virginian proposed that this person was: "To be chosen by the national legislature for the term of seven years."[16] Mr. Randolph's motion passed with eight state delegations (Massachusetts, Connecticut, New York, Delaware, Virginia, North Carolina, South Carolina, and Georgia) in favor and only two (Pennsylvania and Maryland) opposed.[17]

June 8, 1787

On Friday, June 8, 1787, both Elbridge Gerry and Rufus King of Massachusetts submitted a motion to reconsider the selection of the chief executive by the national legislature. It passed by a nine (Massachusetts, New York, New Jersey, Pennsylvania, Delaware, Maryland, Virginia, South Carolina, and Georgia) to two (Connecticut and North Carolina) margin.[18]

June 9, 1787

The very next day (Saturday), Nathaniel Gorham of Massachusetts submitted a motion that the national executive was "to be chosen by the Executives of the individual States."[19] The premise that the governors of the states would be positioned to select an executive leader of the nation was defeated easily. Ten state delegations voted against this resolution (Massachusetts, Connecticut, New York, New Jersey, Pennsylvania, Maryland, Virginia, North Carolina, South Carolina, and Georgia). The Delaware delegation was divided.[20]

The Small States Respond with the New Jersey Plan

On Friday, June 15, 1787, William Patterson of New Jersey responded to the resolutions offered by Edmund Randolph with his own set of ideas.[21] His resolutions were unanimously referred to the Committee of the Whole. With regard to the question of presidential selection, Mr. Patterson proposed that:

> Resolved that the United States in Congress be authorized to elect a federal Executive to consist of _____ persons, to continue in office for the term of _____ years, to receive punctually at stated times a fixed compensation for their services, in which no increase or diminution shall be made so as to affect the persons composing the Executive at the time of such increase or diminution, to be paid out of the federal treasury; to be incapable of holding any other office or appointment during their time of service and for _____ years thereafter; to be ineligible a second time, & removable by Congress on application by a majority of the Executives of the several States; that the Executives besides their general authority to execute the federal acts ought to appoint all federal officers not otherwise provided for, & to direct all military operations; provided that none of the persons composing the federal Executive shall on any occasion take command of any troops, so as personally to conduct any enterprise as General, or in other capacity.[22]

Under the New Jersey Plan, Congress would select an executive council instead of a single chief executive. The resolutions proposed by William Patterson clearly favored states' rights and were strikingly similar to the status quo at the time under the Articles of Confederation and Perpetual Union. Clearly, many small state delegates were distrustful of a powerful executive leader.[23]

July 17, 1787

On Tuesday, July 17, 1787, the Framers took a number of votes pertaining to presidential selection. The Committee of the Whole voted on the following issue: "That a national Executive be instituted to consist of a Single Person."[24] The resolution passed with 10 votes in favor (Massachusetts, Connecticut, New Jersey, Pennsylvania, Delaware, Maryland, Virginia,

North Carolina, South Carolina, and Georgia), and no state delegation was in opposition.[25] The Framers also reconsidered the issue of direct election of the president and voted against it by a nine (Massachusetts, Connecticut, New Jersey, Delaware, Maryland, Virginia, North Carolina, South Carolina, and Georgia) to one (Pennsylvania) vote. Upon doing so, they took another vote on the chief executive: "To be chosen by Electors to be appointed by the several Legislatures of the individual States."[26] The measure failed; it only received two favorable votes (Delaware and Maryland) and eight unfavorable votes (Massachusetts, Connecticut, New Jersey, Pennsylvania, Virginia, North Carolina, South Carolina, and Georgia).[27] After direct election and the selection of electors failed, the Framers revisited the issue of congressional selection of the chief executive by incorporating the following clause: "to be chosen by the national Legislature."[28] In so doing, a unanimous consensus was achieved by the Framers. The chief executive would be selected by the national legislature by a vote of 10 delegations in favor (Massachusetts, Connecticut, New Jersey, Pennsylvania, Delaware, Maryland, Virginia, North Carolina, South Carolina, and Georgia) and zero opposed.[29]

On this day, the Framers considered the issue of term limits with regard to the chief executive and rejected the idea of limiting executive service by a six (Massachusetts, Connecticut, New Jersey, Pennsylvania, Maryland, and Georgia) to four (Delaware, Virginia, North Carolina, and South Carolina) vote margin. Allowing the chief executive to serve during "good behaviour" in *lieu* of a fixed term was also defeated by a six (Massachusetts, Connecticut, Maryland, North Carolina, South Carolina, and Georgia) to four (New Jersey, Pennsylvania, Delaware, and Virginia) tally. Finally, the Framers debated the merits of a presidential term of seven years, and it was narrowly adopted with six votes (Connecticut, New Jersey, Maryland, Virginia, South Carolina, and Georgia) in favor and four votes (Massachusetts, Pennsylvania, Delaware, and North Carolina) in opposition.[30]

It was on this day that Gouverneur Morris of Pennsylvania made a very substantive speech concerning presidential selection. A fascinating and highly informative interpretation of the day's events is provided by Professor William Riker, a noted game theorist, who argued that Gouverneur Morris was a skilled heresthetician in Philadelphia.[31] The Framers were sharing their viewpoints regarding how a single executive should be chosen to enforce the nation's laws. Mr. Morris offered the following insight:

> It is said that in case of an election by the people the populous States will combine & elect whom they please. Just the reverse. The people of such States cannot combine. If their be any combination it must be among their representatives in the Legislature. It is said the people will be led by a few

designing men. This might happen in a small district. It can never happen throughout the continent. In the election of a Govr. of N. York, it sometimes is the case in particular spots, that the activity & intrigues of little partizans are successful, but the general voice of the State is never influenced by such artifices. It is said the multitude will be uninformed. It is true that they would be uninformed of what passed in the Legislative Conclave, if the election were to be made there; but they will not be uninformed of those great & illustrious characters which have merited their esteem & confidence. If the Executive be chosen by the Natl. Legislature, he will not be independent on it; and if not independent, usurpation & tyranny on the part of the Legislature will be the consequence. This was the case in England in the last Century. It has been the case in Holland, where their Senates have engrossed all power. It has been the case every where. He was surprised that an election by the people at large should ever have been likened to the polish election of the first Magistrate. An election by the Legislature will bear a real likeness to the election by the Diet of Poland. The great must be the electors in both cases, and the corruption & cabal wch are known to characterize the one would soon find their way into the other. Appointments made by numerous bodies, are always worse than those made by single responsible individuals, or by the people at large.[32]

Gouverneur Morris boldly declared on that day that "[i]f the Legislature elect, it will be the work of intrigue, of cabal, and of faction: it will be like the election of a pope by a conclave of cardinals; real merit will rarely be the title to the appointment."[33] Thus Mr. Morris introduced an idea to his colleagues who, at this point in Philadelphia, appeared to endorse legislative selection of the chief executive. He suggested that legislative selection of the president would yield a dependent executive, beholden to the legislative branch of government. Such an arrangement would clearly violate the principles of separation of powers and checks and balances.

July 19, 1787

On this Thursday, the Framers reconsidered some issues regarding presidential selection, and the delegates appeared to have been swayed, at least to some measurable extent, by Gouverneur Morris's points made two days earlier. The Framers supported a resolution providing for presidential selection by electors by a six (Connecticut, New Jersey, Pennsylvania, Delaware, Maryland, and Virginia) to three (North Carolina, South Carolina, and Georgia) margin with one state (Massachusetts) divided.[34] The motion specified that the chief executive was:

to be chosen by Electors appointed for that purpose by the Legislatures of the States, in the following proportion *One person* from each State whose numbers, according to the ratio fixed in the resolution, shall not exceed 100,000—*Two* from each of the others, whose numbers shall not exceed 300,000—and *Three* from each of the rest.[35]

More support was garnered with a subsequent motion that simply read that the executive was: "To be chosen by electors appointed for that purpose by the Legislatures of the States."[36] The eight state delegations in favor of this measure included Massachusetts, Connecticut, New Jersey, Pennsylvania, Delaware, Maryland, North Carolina, and Georgia. Virginia and South Carolina rejected the motion.[37]

The Framers also revisited the issue of fixed presidential terms. A seven-year term was rejected with three states (New Jersey, South Carolina, and Georgia) in favor, five (Connecticut, Pennsylvania, Delaware, Maryland, and Virginia) opposed, and two (Massachusetts and North Carolina) divided. A six-year term was more palatable, however, by a nine (Massachusetts, Connecticut, New Jersey, Pennsylvania, Maryland, Virginia, North Carolina, South Carolina, and Georgia) to one (Delaware) margin. Term limits were rejected by an eight (Massachusetts, Connecticut, New Jersey, Pennsylvania, Delaware, Maryland, Virginia, and Georgia) to two (North and South Carolina) vote.[38]

July 23, 1787

On this Monday, the New Hampshire delegates (John Langdon and Nicholas Gilman) arrived and took their seats at the Convention.[39] The Framers decided to once again reconsider presidential selection by electors by a seven (New Hampshire, Massachusetts, Connecticut, Delaware, North Carolina, South Carolina, and Georgia) to three (Pennsylvania, Maryland, and Virginia) margin.[40]

July 24, 1787

The following day (Tuesday), the delegates voted seven (New Hampshire, Massachusetts, New Jersey, Delaware, North Carolina, South Carolina, and Georgia) to four (Connecticut, Pennsylvania, Maryland, and Virginia) in favor of presidential selection by the national legislature once again.[41] The Framers were obviously profoundly perplexed about how to select a president in a proper manner. This truly is depicted in their voting behavior. On July 17, they opted for presidential selection by the national legislature. Two days later, they voted in favor of presidential selection by electors. Then five days later, they voted for legislative selection again.[42] This pattern of relative indecisiveness on the matter of presidential selection would continue for some time in Philadelphia.

July 25, 1787

On Wednesday, the very next day, the Framers rejected presidential selection by the national legislature by a seven (Massachusetts, New Jersey, Delaware, Virginia, North Carolina, South Carolina, and Georgia) to four (New Hampshire, Connecticut, Pennsylvania, and Maryland) vote.[43] Consequently, Oliver Ellsworth of Connecticut proposed a resolution that the chief executive would be initially selected by the national legislature. If, however, the president was eligible to serve another term, electors would be selected by the state legislatures to determine whether or not the incumbent president deserved an additional term in office. In this manner, Mr. Ellsworth contended that the chief executive would be independent of the legislative branch. His motion was rejected by a seven (Massachusetts, New Jersey, Delaware, Virginia, North Carolina, South Carolina, and Georgia) to four (New Hampshire, Connecticut, Pennsylvania, and Maryland) vote. Thus, some consistency on July 25 regarding presidential selection had evolved in Philadelphia.[44] It would not last very long, however.

July 26, 1787

The repudiation of legislative selection of the president from the previous day was reversed 24 hours later by the Framers on this Thursday. The following resolution was passed by a six (New Hampshire, Connecticut, New Jersey, North Carolina, South Carolina, and Georgia) to three (Pennsylvania, Delaware, and Maryland) vote. The vote for the Virginia delegation was divided:[45]

> Resolved That a national Executive be instituted to consist of a Single Person to be chosen by a national Legislature for the term of seven years to be ineligible a second time.[46]

It was on this day that George Mason of Virginia provided a summary of what had transpired in Philadelphia with regard to selection of the national executive:

> In every stage of the Question relative to the Executive, the difficulty of the subject and the diversity of opinions concerning it have appeared. Nor have any of the modes of constituting that department been satisfactory. 1. It has been proposed that the election should be made by the people at large; that is that an act which ought to be performed by those who know most of Eminent characters, & qualifications, should be performed by those who know least. 2. that the election should be made by the Legislatures of the States. 3. by the Executives of the States. Agst these modes also strong objections have been urged. 4. It has been proposed that the election should be made

by Electors chosen by the people for that purpose. This was first agreed to: But on further consideration has been rejected. 5. Since which, the mode of Mr. Williamson, requiring each freeholder to vote for several candidates has been proposed. This seemed like many other propositions, to carry a plausible face, but on closer inspection is liable to fatal objections. A popular election (in any form), as Mr. Gerry has observed, would throw the appointment into the hands of the Cincinnati, a Society for the members of which he had a great respect; but which he never wished to have a preponderating influence in the Govt. 6. Another expedient was proposed by Mr. Dickenson, which is liable to so palpable & material an inconvenience that he had little (doubt) of its being by this time rejected by himself. It would exclude every man who happened not to be popular within his own State; tho' the causes of his local unpopularity might be of such a nature as to recommend him to the States at large. 7. Among other expedients, a lottery has been introduced. But as the tickets do not appear to be in much demand, it will probably, not be carried on, and nothing therefore need be said on that subject. After reviewing all these various modes, he was led to conclude—that an election by the Natl Legislature as originally proposed, was the best. If it was liable to objections, it was liable to fewer than any other. He conceived at the same time that a second election ought to be absolutely prohibited. Having for this primary object, for the pole star of his political conduct, the preservation of the rights of the people, he held it as an essential point, as the very palladium of Civil liberty, that the great offices of State, and particularly the Executive should at fixed periods return to the masses from which they were at first taken, in order that they may feel & respect those rights & interests, Which are again to be personally valuable to them.[47]

This is late July in Philadelphia, and the Framers are weeks away from completing their objective. Suffice it to say at this point that the architects of the new republic were deeply divided on the question of presidential selection and did not all rally around the concept of electors.

The Committee of Detail

The Philadelphia Convention adjourned from July 26 to August 6 to allow the Committee of Detail to engage in its activities.[48] Five delegates were selected to serve on this committee, which was charged with the task of preparing a draft of the Constitution. John Rutledge of South Carolina was the chair, and the other committee members included Oliver Ellsworth, Nathaniel Gorham, Edmund Randolph, and James Wilson. No record of the proceedings of the Committee of Detail were kept.[49]

On Monday, August 6, the draft of the Constitution was presented to the delegates by the committee chair. With regard to the executive, the committee members presented their recommendations to the Committee of the Whole:

The Executive Power of the United States shall be vested in a single person. His stile shall be "The President of the United States of America;" and his title shall be, "His Excellency". He shall be elected by ballot by the Legislature. He shall hold his office during the term of seven years; but shall not be elected a second time.[50]

The Framers would not scrutinize this part of the Committee of Detail's report until August 24. By late August, the Framers were a very weary lot of individuals who were fatigued and eager to return to their families.[51]

August 24, 1787

The Framers voted on this Friday on a proposal to change executive selection from the national legislature to the will of the people. It was rejected by the delegates by a nine (New Hampshire, Massachusetts, Connecticut, New Jersey, Maryland, Virginia, North Carolina, South Carolina, and Georgia) to two (Pennsylvania and Delaware) vote.[52] They also reconsidered, yet again, the feasibility of creating a somewhat vague system of electors empowered to select the nation's chief executive. The result of this vote is indicative of the Framer's indecision: five (Connecticut, New Jersey, Pennsylvania, Delaware, and Virginia) affirmation votes and six (New Hampshire, Massachusetts, Maryland, North Carolina, South Carolina, and Georgia) negative votes.[53]

August 31, 1787

One Friday later, the Framers decided to create a Committee of Eleven (one delegate per state still in attendance) to address tabled issues and committee reports that had not been acted upon. Those commissioned to serve on this committee included Abraham Baldwin (Georgia), David Brearley (New Jersey), Pierce Butler (South Carolina), Daniel Carrol (Maryland), John Dickinson (Delaware), Nicholas Gilman (New Hampshire), Rufus King (Massachusetts), James Madison (Virginia), Gouverneur Morris (Pennsylvania), Roger Sherman (Connecticut), and Hugh Williamson (North Carolina).[54] As history has demonstrated, the Framers were 17 days away from finishing their business and had still not agreed on how a president would be selected. It was up to the Committee of Eleven to figure out this complicated matter.[55]

September 4, 1787

David Brearley was the chair of this important committee. On behalf of the committee, he issued a report on this Tuesday. In it, the Committee of

Eleven recommended to the Convention that the president be selected by electors chosen by state legislatures:

> He shall hold his office during the term of four years, and together with the vice-President, chosen for the same term, be elected in the following manner, viz. Each State shall appoint in such manner as its Legislature may direct, a number of electors equal to the whole number of Senators and members of the House of Representatives, to which the State may be entitled in the Legislature. The Electors shall meet in their respective States, and vote by ballot for two persons, of whom one at least shall not be an inhabitant of the same State with themselves; and they shall make a list of all the persons voted for, and of the number of votes for each, which list they shall sign and certify and transmit sealed to the Seat of the. Genl. Government, directed to the President of the Senate—The President of the Senate shall in that House open all the certificates; and the votes shall be then & there counted. The Person having the greatest number of votes shall be President, if such number be a majority of that of the electors; and if there be more than one who have such a majority, and have an equal number of votes, then the Senate shall immediately choose by ballot one of them for President: but if no person have a majority. then from the five highest on the list, the Senate shall choose by ballot the President. And in every case after the choice of the President, the person having the greatest number of votes shall be vice-president: but if there should remain two or more who have equal votes, the Senate shall choose from them the vice-President. The Legislature may determine the time of choosing and assembling the Electors, and the manner of certifying and transmitting their votes.[56]

This resolution by the Committee of Eleven was clearly a wide-ranging compromise of the many different visions that the Framers had concerning executive selection. Using electors would satisfy some who wanted a discernible role for the people in electing a president. Not permitting congressional selection of the president would also result in additional supporters, particularly those who believed in the notion of separation of powers relevant to that time period. Having the number of electors equal to all senators and representatives would be attractive to the large state delegations. In addition, this formula also gave the southern states extra electoral votes due to the three-fifths compromise. Small state delegates presumably were appeased because each state was afforded equality by the Framers in the U.S. Senate as two senators were allocated per state, regardless of population size.[57]

September 6, 1787

On Thursday, the delegates voted 9 (New Hampshire, Massachusetts, Connecticut, New Jersey, Pennsylvania, Delaware, Maryland, Virginia, and

Georgia) to 2 (North and South Carolina) in favor of presidential selection by electors.[58] In addition, the Framers changed the venue of contingent elections from the Senate to the House of Representatives by a 10 to 1 margin (the Delaware delegation was in opposition).[59] If a president were to be selected by the House of Representatives, each state delegation would have one vote. This provision was endorsed by 10 of the voting delegations at this time and only opposed by Delaware.[60]

September 17, 1787

On September 8 (Saturday), a Committee of Style and Arrangement was created to revise the style and arrangement of the Constitution. The appointees included William Johnson (Connecticut), Rufus King (Massachusetts), James Madison (Virginia), Gouverneur Morris (Pennsylvania), and Alexander Hamilton (New York).[61] The committee issued its report on Wednesday, September 12.[62] On the concluding day of the Philadelphia Convention, Monday, September 17, the Constitution was endorsed by all 11 state delegations that could vote (Rhode Island and New York excepted).[63] The Framers would return to their homes and proceed with the debate about ratifying the document in question.

SUMMARY

The Framers of the Constitution were deeply troubled about the issue of presidential selection. This is reflected in the many votes with different outcomes taken throughout the Convention. Because the Framers broke into the Committee of the Whole, they could revisit any issue that they desired. They were obviously compelled to do so in Philadelphia with regard to presidential selection because they truly did not come to any consensus on the matter. The fact that they ultimately decided to create the Electoral College is summarized brilliantly by the great political scientist, Robert Dahl:

> Every solution seemed worse than the rest. The arrangement they finally cobbled together at the last minute was adopted more out of desperation, perhaps, than out of any great confidence in its success. So why did the delegates finally give their approval to the electoral college? Probably the best answer to our question would be: the Framers settled on an electoral college because they had run out of alternatives.[64]

Thus, the mechanism that still is in operation today to elect the president of the United States, the longest running democracy on the planet, was created by a group of men in 1787 who were utterly baffled about the appropriate means to select a chief executive and who were clearly fearful of executive tyranny given the recent experience of Americans during the oppressive reign of King George III. Contemporary Americans also must consider that the Framers did not envision the evolution of political parties either. Thus, in a time period where elites did not want to give the people too much power because they feared mob rule, where slavery still existed, where women had little by way of rights, and where America had no political parties, the Electoral College was established.

As discussed in Chapter 1, democratization has been a key hallmark in America's political development. Civil liberties have been extended precisely because the world of the late 18th century has changed. The right to vote was extended first to those white males who did not own property, and then to non-Christians, African Americans, women, and young people. Direct election was provided to the people in the case of U.S. senators almost a century ago. That same liberty has been denied to Americans throughout the existence of the republic to date with regard to presidential selection, resulting in "wrong winners" (i.e., the winner of the popular vote lost in the Electoral College) in 1824, 1876, 1888, and 2000; it almost occurred in a number of other presidential elections as well.[65]

Well over 700 proposed amendments to modify or abolish the Electoral College have been introduced in Congress during the nation's history. This is the most popular subject of constitutional reform, yet little has changed since the Framers drafted the Constitution.[66] In the 21st century, the people of the United States of America should have the right, as well as the responsibility, to select their own president. More by way of discourse on this subject will be forthcoming by way of conclusion in Chapter 6.

Chapter 5

MONEY AND ELECTIONS
IN AMERICA

Presidential and congressional campaign expenditures have increased significantly and show no signs of decelerating at any point in the future. As one political scientist noted: "The problem of money in politics will remain with us for the foreseeable future."[1] The 2008 presidential election was historic by many criteria. Not only did Barack Obama become the first African American leader elected president in the nation's history, but he also was the first sitting U.S. senator to win the presidency since John F. Kennedy in 1960. He broke fund raising records, won by a sizable margin, and he raised and spent a lot of money to capture the top prize.

MONEY IN PRESIDENTIAL ELECTIONS

Included in Table 5.1 is a delineation of total contributions to presidential candidates from 1976–2008.[2] In 1976, $171 million was contributed to all presidential candidates. In 2008, 32 years later, over $1.7 billion was given to all presidential candidates, a tenfold increase from the contest ultimately between Gerald Ford and Jimmy Carter. By this historical measure, in 2040, *ceteris paribus*, $17 billion will be collected by all U.S. presidential candidates. The presidential election of 2008 marked the first time in U.S. history that candidates raised more than $1 billion.[3]

While many citizens perceive a link between campaign donations and how an elected official actually votes on public policy issues, political scientists generally contend that lobbyists seek to gain access to elected officials, particularly the members of Congress at the federal level.[4] Whether

Table 5.1
Total Contributions to Presidential Candidates, 1976–2008

Presidential Election Year	Total Contributions to Presidential Candidates	Major Political Party Nominees
1976	$171,000,000	Jimmy Carter (D) Gerald Ford (R)
1980	$161,900,000	Jimmy Carter (D) Ronald Reagan (R)
1984	$202,000,000	Walter Mondale (D) Ronald Reagan (R)
1988	$324,400,000	Michael Dukakis (D) George H. W. Bush (R)
1992	$331,100,000	Bill Clinton (D) George H. W. Bush (R)
1996	$425,700,000	Bill Clinton (D) Robert Dole (R)
2000	$528,900,000	Al Gore (D) George W. Bush (R)
2004	$880,500,000	John Kerry (D) George W. Bush (R)
2008	$1,748,800,000	Barack Obama (D) John McCain (R)

Source: Center for Responsive Politics. 2009. Presidential Fundraising and Spending, 1976–2008. Accessed October 18, 2009, from: http://www.opensecrets.org/pres08/totals.php?cycle=2004.

or not access leads to policy advocacy is another issue altogether. Presumably, individuals and lobbying officials generally donate money to candidates with similar policy and ideological viewpoints. While some elected officials may alter their voting behavior due to political contributions, it is highly unlikely that members of Congress *en masse* engage in this practice. Yet analysts representing the nonpartisan and nonprofit organization Public Agenda provide an encompassing summary of the current practice of political contributions on the part of supporters:

> With all that money floating around, the natural question is what (or who) is being bought? Corporations and interest groups who give money say what they're most interested in is "access"—that giving money increases their chances of being listened to when their cause is being debated in Congress. Sometimes, also, wealthy people give in order to promote ideas that

they're interested in, such as when Ross Perot spent his own money to run for president, or the way billionaire George Soros funds ballot referendums to change drug laws. Many critics of campaign finance reform plans argue that there's nothing wrong with groups of like-minded people getting together to elect candidates who agree with them, and to lobby them once they're in office.[5]

The aggregate amount of money raised and spent in congressional elections, not unlike the case of presidential campaigns, is the subject of a great deal of controversy in terms of its cumulative effect on the democratic process.

MONEY IN CONGRESSIONAL ELECTIONS

Included in Table 5.2 are some critical financial and incumbency data for every federal election from 1990–2008.[6] With regard to House elections, some things have not changed from 20 years ago. The vast majority of all incumbents (from either party) are routinely reelected to the rate of about 95 percent from one election to another. Turnover exists in the House primarily due to voluntary retirements as well as the pursuit of higher offices. Winners typically spend much more than losers, and that will not likely change due to the many advantages that incumbents have over challengers, including name recognition and robust end-of-the year balances after the election has already taken place. A serious contender for a U.S. House seat faces the daunting reality that, on average, she or he has to raise and spend about $1.5 million in contemporary terms. That means that a lot of time has to be dedicated to the sheer act of fund raising and less on more important substantive matters.

About $4 million was the average amount spent for a winning Senate campaign 20 years ago. It is now more than twice that figure; not surprising, losers spend a great deal more as well. Similar to their House counterparts, Senate incumbents almost always prevail as well. Well over 80 percent of the time incumbents of both parties are retained by the voters in their respective states, undoubtedly due to some of the same reasons why this is the prevailing practice in the House. Senate campaigns, on average, are a lot more expensive to run and operate than most House campaigns. This requires a great deal of invested energy into fund raising on the part of successful senators because, on average, they will need to raise and spend $8–9 million to secure the job in today's world.

(Text continues on page 94.)

Table 5.2
Congressional Campaign Expenditures, 1990–2008

	U.S. House of Representatives			
	1990	1992	1994	1996
Average Winner Spent	$407,556	$543,599	$516,126	$673,739
Average Loser Spent	$116,665	$201,263	$238,715	$265,675
Most Expensive Campaign	$1,707,539	$5,435,177	$2,621,479	$5,577,715
Least Expensive Winning Campaign	$6,766	$6,624	$27,554	$66,071
Incumbents Seeking Reelection	406	368	387	383
Number of Incumbents Reelected	390	325	349	360
Incumbents' Reelection Rates	96%	88%	90%	94%
Average Winner's End-of-Year Balance	$156,821	$73,496	$81	$118,446
Biggest End-of-Year Balance	$1,859,603	$2,116,689	$2,306,513	$5,051,292
	1998	2000	2002	2004
Average Winner Spent	$650,428	$840,300	$898,184	$1,034,224
Average Loser Spent	$210,614	$307,121	$283,933	$279,267
Most Expensive Campaign	$7,578,716	$6,964,933	$8,150,237	$5,013,947
Least Expensive Winning Campaign	$34,258	$56,828	$81,357	$49,004
Incumbents Seeking Reelection	402	403	398	404

	1998	2000	2002	2004
Number of Incumbents Reelected	395	394	382	395
Incumbents' Reelection Rates	98%	98%	96%	98%
Average Winner's End-of-Year Balance	$190,978	$272,817	$307,187	$369,375
Biggest End-of-Year Balance	$2,643,806	$2,360,082	$2,563,095	$4,515,955

	2006	2008
Average Winner Spent	$1,253,031	$1,372,539
Average Loser Spent	$622,348	$492,928
Most Expensive Campaign	$8,112,752	$7,323,502
Least Expensive Winning Campaign	$182,375	$94,049
Incumbents Seeking Reelection	404	403
Number of Incumbents Reelected	380	380
Incumbents' Reelection Rates	94%	94%
Average Winner's End-of-Year Balance	$363,768	$412,376
Biggest End-of-Year Balance	$5,119,677	$4,996,801

U.S. Senate[1]				
	1990	1992	1994	1996
Average Winner Spent	$3,870,621	$3,930,638	$4,569,940	$4,692,110
Average Loser Spent	$1,674,658	$2,034,980	$3,426,509	$2,773,756

(continued)

Table 5.2
Congressional Campaign Expenditures, 1990–2008 *(continued)*

	U.S. Senate[1]			
	1990	*1992*	*1994*	*1996*
Most Expensive Campaign	$17,761,579	$11,550,958	$29,969,695	$14,587,143
Least Expensive Winning Campaign	$533,632	$875,675	$1,020,334	$953,572
Incumbents Seeking Reelection	32	29	29	21
Number of Incumbents Reelected	31	24	24	19
Incumbents' Reelection Rates	97%	83%	83%	91%
Average Winner's End-of-Year Balance	$465,153	$193,749	$-149,639	$197,577
Biggest End-of-Year Balance	$4,147,378	$1,756,483	$1,568,900	$980,751
	1998	*2000*	*2002*	*2004*
Average Winner Spent	$5,227,761	$7,266,576	$5,373,841	$7,840,976
Average Loser Spent	$2,839,813	$3,864,638	$3,375,875	$3,628,332
Most Expensive Campaign	$27,159,681	$63,209,506	$13,688,920	$28,952,326
Least Expensive Winning Campaign	$1,116,112	$630,965	$1,114,028	$1,326,661
Incumbents Seeking Reelection	29	29	28	26
Number of Incumbents Reelected	26	23	24	25
Incumbents' Reelection Rates	90%	79%	86%	96%

	1998	2000	2002	2004
Average Winner's End-of-Year Balance	$90,022	$642,801	$512,999	$1,560,730
Biggest End-of-Year Balance	$4,559,425	$4,622,229	$3,256,828	$11,246,330

	2006	2008
Average Winner Spent	$9,635,370	$8,531,267
Average Loser Spent	$7,406,678	$4,130,078
Most Expensive Campaign	$40,828,991	$21,821,755
Least Expensive Winning Campaign	$1,529,370	$1,981,441
Incumbents Seeking Reelection	29	30
Number of Incumbents Reelected	23	25
Incumbents' Reelection Rates	79%	83%
Average Winner's End-of-Year Balance	$1,462,024	$995,766
Biggest End-of-Year Balance	$11,021,087	$3,988,104

[1] Figures cover full six-year cycle for Senate incumbents.

Source: Center for Responsive Politics. 2009. Election Stats. Accessed October 18, 2009, from: http://www.opensecrets.org/bigpicture/elec_stats.php.

HISTORY OF CAMPAIGN FINANCE REFORM
IN THE UNITED STATES

Throughout most of America's history candidates of both major parties depended almost exclusively on large contributions from wealthy private donors to finance their campaigns. These contributions were secret and sometimes downright illegal, and citizens knew very little about who gave how much money to political candidates. This reality prompted reformers to raise serious concerns about the sheer conduct of elections in a democratic society. Could elected officials respond to the greater public good when they were receiving large amounts of money from specific individuals and groups?[7]

President Theodore Roosevelt proposed that the campaign finance system in federal elections be reformed in 1905. In his fifth State of the Union address, he declared:

> In my last annual message I said:
> "The power of the Government to protect the integrity of the elections of its own officials is inherent and has been recognized and affirmed by repeated declarations of the Supreme Court. There is no enemy of free government more dangerous and none so insidious as the corruption of the electorate. No one defends or excuses corruption, and it would seem to follow that none would oppose vigorous measures to eradicate it. I recommend the enactment of a law directed against bribery and corruption in Federal elections. The details of such a law may be safely left to the wise discretion of the Congress, but it should go as far as under the Constitution it is possible to go, and should include severe penalties against him who gives or receives a bribe intended to influence his act or opinion as an elector; and provisions for the publication not only of the expenditures for nominations and elections of all candidates, but also of all contributions received and expenditures made by political committees."[8]

President Roosevelt reiterated his premise that federal intervention was needed to ensure the integrity of political campaigns and the electoral process:

> I desire to repeat this recommendation. In political campaigns in a country as large and populous as ours it is inevitable that there should be much expense of an entirely legitimate kind. This, of course, means that many contributions, and some of them of large size, must be made, and, as a matter of fact, in any big political contest such contributions are always made on both sides. It is entirely proper to give and receive them, unless there is an improper motive connected with either gift or reception. If they are extorted by any kind of pressure or promise, express or implied, direct or indirect, in the way of favor or immunity, then the giving or receiving becomes not only improper

but criminal. It will undoubtedly be difficult, as a matter of practical detail, to shape an act which shall guard with reasonable certainty against such misconduct; but if it is possible to secure by law the full and verified publication in detail of all the sums contributed to and expended by the candidates or committees of any political parties, the result cannot but be wholesome. All contributions by corporations to any political committee or for any political purpose should be forbidden by law; directors should not be permitted to use stockholders' money for such purposes; and, moreover, a prohibition of this kind would be, as far as it went, an effective method of stopping the evils aimed at in corrupt practices acts. Not only should both the National and the several State Legislatures forbid any officer of a corporation from using the money of the corporation in or about any election, but they should also forbid such use of money in connection with any legislation save by the employment of counsel in public manner for distinctly legal services.[9]

Clearly, reformers in the early 20th century believed that undue influence on the democratic process in the form of substantial campaign contributions to political candidates had to be regulated by Congress in order to protect the greater public good. Ironically, it was controversy surrounding the 1904 presidential election that led to the first organized movement for campaign finance reform.[10]

Tillman Act (1907)

In 1904, Judge Alton Parker, the Chief Judge of the New York Court of Appeals and the Democratic presidential nominee, alleged that corporations were providing President Theodore Roosevelt with campaign gifts in order to buy influence with the administration. The president denied the charges, but it became known that officials from several major companies made large contributions to the Republican party. This is the context of the President's call for campaign finance reform in 1905 and 1906. Congress responded in 1907 by passing the Tillman Act. This law prohibited any contributions by corporations and national banks to federal political campaigns.[11]

Publicity Act of 1910 (The Federal Corrupt Practices Act)

Shortly before the 1910 elections (the midterm election during William Howard Taft's tenure as president), the Republican majority passed a bill that required nothing more than postelection reports of the receipts and expenditures of national party committees or committees operating in two or more states. This bill initially only applied to the U.S. House of Representatives as members were directly elected by the people and the Seventeenth Amendment had not been ratified yet. This law did not require any disclosure prior to an election. Amendments to this act in 1911 improved disclosure and established the first spending limits for federal campaigns. Disclosure was extended to include primaries and conventions, and the amendments required preelection as well as postelection disclosure of campaign finances by both Senate and House campaigns. The law limited House expenditures to a total of $5,000 and Senate expenditures to $10,000 or the amount established by state law (whichever was less).[12]

These spending limits, however, quickly became controversial and became the subject of judicial scrutiny. Later in 1925, the act was amended again and required that financial disclosure reports be made quarterly. It also established a requirement that any contribution over $100 be reported. Senate campaign spending limits were raised to $25,000. The law, however, provided no regulatory authority to establish the manner of reporting or its disclosure to the people, and no penalties for failure to comply were created.[13]

Newberry v. United States (1921)

In 1918, Truman Newberry, a Michigan Republican candidate for U.S. Senate, defeated the legendary automobile manufacturer Henry Ford in a hotly contested primary. Mr. Newberry allegedly spent about more than $100,000 in his effort to secure the nomination.[14] This is more than 25 times the limit established by Michigan law. Under the state's law, candidates for federal office could not spend more than 25 percent of his/her anticipated federal salary for the purposes of securing the nomination and another 25 percent of his/her anticipated federal salary on the general election. This amounted to $3,750 at the time.[15] Mr. Newberry was found guilty in the state courts. He appealed his conviction to the U.S. Supreme Court, and it was overturned by the justices.[16]

Justice James McReynolds wrote for the Court's majority. He contended that under the U.S. Constitution, Congress did not have the power to regulate primary elections or political party nomination processes:

> We cannot conclude that authority to control party primaries or conventions for designating candidates was bestowed on Congress by the grant of power to regulate the manner of holding elections. The fair intendment of the words does not extend so far; the framers of the Constitution did not ascribe to them any such meaning. Nor is this control necessary in order to effectuate the power expressly granted. On the other hand, its exercise would interfere with purely domestic affairs of the state and infringe upon liberties reserved to the people. It should not be forgotten that, exercising inherent police power, the state may suppress whatever evils may be incident to primary or convention. As each house shall be the judge of the elections, qualifications and returns of its own members, and as Congress may by law

regulate the times, places and manner of holding elections, the national government is not without power to protect itself against corruption, fraud or other malign influences.[17]

The Court's majority clearly relied upon a very narrow interpretation of Congress' authority to regulate campaign finance in the federal electoral process. This interpretation would remain the law of the land for another 20 years.[18]

The Hatch Act (1939)

The Hatch Act restricted the ability of federal employees to participate in partisan politics. It prohibited civil service workers from soliciting campaign contributions, which had the overall effect of removing a major source of revenue for state and local party organizations. In 1940, amendments were added to the Act to restrict the amount of money donated to political campaigns. Individuals were limited to $5,000 per year on contributions to federal candidates or national party committees and $3,000,000 on the total amount that could be received or spent by a party committee operating in two or more states.[19]

Like the earlier regulations, these restrictions had little effect on political giving by the people. Donors could still give large sums of money by giving to multiple committees or by making contributions through state and local party organizations, which were not subject to the $5,000 limit.[20]

United States v. Classic (1941)

In this case, the justices reviewed the precedent that was established in *Newberry v. U.S.* (1921). In *Newberry*, it was thought that the justices determined that Congress did not have the authority under Article I, Section 4 of the Constitution to regulate primary elections. In 1941, however, the justices through Harlan Fiske Stone had a different interpretation of congressional power under Article I:

[W]e think that the authority of Congress, given by Section 4, includes the authority to regulate primary elections when, as in this case, they are a step in the exercise by the people of their choice of representatives in Congress. . . . In *Newberry v. United States*, four justices of this Court were of opinion that the term "elections" in Section 4 of Article I did not embrace a primary election, since that procedure was unknown to the framers. A fifth Justice, who with them pronounced the judgment of the Court, was of opinion that a primary, held under a law enacted before the adoption of the Seventeenth Amendment, for the nomination of candidates for Senator, was not an election of Senators by the state legislatures to which their election had been committed by Article I, Section 3. The remaining four Justices were of the opinion that a primary election for the choice of candidates for Senator or Representative were elections subject to regulation by Congress within the meaning of Section 4 of Article I. The question then has not been prejudged by any decision of this Court.[21]

In other words, it was the contention of Justice Stone that the *Newberry* Court had been deeply divided on the issue about Congress's ability to regulate primaries and that no majority had ruled one way or the other. As a result, the justices maintained that Congress did have the authority to regulate primaries wherever state law made them part of the election process and wherever they effectively determined the outcome of the general election.[22]

The members of Congress did not address the issue of campaign finance reform for almost 30 years following World War II:

> A change in campaign funding during the postwar era that was even more important than PACs was a result not of adaptation to the law but of a change in the style of campaigning. While party organizations remained an important source of revenue, campaigns became increasingly candidate-based. Candidates for federal office established their own committees and raised their own funds. At the same time, television was becoming an essential means of political communication, significantly increasing the costs of seeking federal office. The rising cost of campaigns renewed concerns about the campaign finance system and the role of wealth in national elections. Yet despite the concerns, Congress took no action. The only serious gesture made toward reform between World War II and the Vietnam War era was President John F. Kennedy's decision to form a Commission on Campaign Costs to explore problems in the system and develop legislative proposals. The Commission's 1962 report offered a comprehensive program of reform, including such innovative ideas as a system of public matching funds for presidential candidates. However, Congress was not receptive to the president's proposals, and no effort was made to resurrect those ideas after his assassination.[23]

By the late 1960s, many members of Congress became increasingly concerned about the escalating costs of political campaigns for federal office. Some were focused on the reality that wealthy challengers might have the resources needed to beat them in a largely media-based campaign. Democrats became particularly attentive to the rising costs of campaigns, as Republicans had raised considerably more funds than them and had spent more than twice as much as the Democrats in the 1968 presidential election, where Richard Nixon (R) defeated Hubert Humphrey (D) by a very close margin. With this renewed interest in campaign finance reform, the Federal Election Campaign Act of 1971 was passed by Congress.

Federal Election Campaign Act (FECA) of 1971

The Federal Election Campaign Act of 1971 was signed into law by President Richard Nixon on February 7, 1972. It went into effect 60 days later on April 7, 1972. A twofold approach to campaign finance reform was attempted under this legislation. First, the law established detailed spending limits for all federal campaigns. Second, the act imposed strict public disclosure procedures on federal candidates and political committees.[24]

In terms of spending limits, the act imposed ceilings on personal contributions by candidates and their immediate families of $50,000 for presidential and vice presidential candidates, $35,000 for Senate candidates, and $25,000 for House candidates. It limited the amounts candidates for federal office could spend on radio, television, cable television, newspapers, magazines, and automated telephone systems in any primary, runoff, special, or general election to $50,000 or $0.10 times the voting age population of the jurisdiction covered by the election, whichever was greater. Additionally, no more than 60 percent of a candidate's overall media spending could be devoted to radio and television advertising. These limits applied separately to primary and general elections and were indexed to increases in the consumer price index.[25]

In the area of disclosure, the law required every candidate or political committee active in a federal campaign to file a quarterly report of receipts and expenditures. These reports had to list any contribution or expenditure of $100 or more and include the name, address, occupation, and principal place of business of the donor or recipient. During election years, any contribution of $5,000 or more had to be reported within 48 hours of its receipt; all reports had to be made available to the public within 48 hours of receipt.[26] In the wake of Watergate and reports of widespread financial abuse in the Nixon reelection campaign of 1972, Congress revised the federal campaign finance system in 1974 by passing the Federal Election Campaign Act Amendments of 1974.[27]

Federal Election Campaign Act Amendments of 1974

Although the 1974 amendments to the FECA technically amended the original law, very few of the original provisions remained intact. The amendments were signed into law by President Gerald Ford on October 15, 1974, and represented the most comprehensive reform of the campaign finance system ever enacted.[28]

New spending ceilings were established with this law. Senate candidates could spend no more than $100,000 or $.08 times the voting age population of the state in a primary election, whichever was greater, and no more than $150,000 or $0.12 times the voting age population in a general election, whichever was greater. House candidates in multidistrict states were limited to $70,000 in the primary and the same amount in the general election. Presidential candidates were restricted to $10 million in the nomination campaign and $20 million in the general election. All of the ceilings were indexed to reflect increases in the Consumer Price Index, and candidates could spend an additional 20 percent of the spending limit for fund raising costs.[29]

National party committees also became restricted in terms of how much they could spend on behalf of candidates. Officials representing such organizations were limited to $10,000 per candidate in House general elections; $20,000 in Senate general elections; and $2.9 million for their presidential candidate. A major political party committee (a party whose candidate received more than 25% of the popular vote in the previous election) was limited to $2 million in convention expenditures. Minor parties (a party whose candidate received between 5% and 25% of the vote in the previous election) were limited to lesser amounts.[30]

In order to eliminate the potential corruptive influence of large donors, the FECA amendments in 1974 established strict limits on individuals who wished to contribute to political campaigns. An individual could contribute no more than $1,000 per candidate in any primary, runoff, or general election. Individuals could not exceed $25,000 in annual aggregate contributions to all federal candidates. Political action committees were limited to $5,000 per candidate per election but had no aggregate limits; independent expenditures made on behalf of a candidate were limited to $1,000 a year, and cash donations in excess of $100 were prohibited.[31]

The Federal Election Commission (FEC) was established by this law. The FEC is an independent agency charged with the mission of administering and enforcing campaign finance regulations. The law stipulated that the Commission would be bipartisan and consist of six members. To assist it, members of Congress tightened the FECA's disclosure and reporting requirements. All candidates were required to establish one central campaign committee through which all contributions and expenditures had to be reported. They were also required to disclose the bank depositories that were authorized to receive campaign funds.[32]

Finally, the bill mandated the creation of a public financing system for presidential election campaigns financed from the tax checkoff receipts deposited in the Presidential Election Campaign Fund. If candidates agreed to eschew private donations, they could receive the full amount authorized under the law for the general election ($20 million). Minor party candidates could receive a fraction of this amount, with the size of the funding commensurate with the proportion of the popular vote received in the previous election compared with the average vote of the major parties. In the primary election, presidential candidates were eligible for public matching funds if they fulfilled certain fund raising requirements. To qualify, a candidate was required to raise at least $5,000 in contributions of $250 or less in at least 20 states.[33] Almost immediately, key provisions of this law were challenged as unconstitutional in a lawsuit filed by Senator James Buckley (R-New York) against the secretary of the U.S. Senate, Francis Valeo.

Buckley v. Valeo (1976)

Given the context of the times present in the early to mid-1970s, members of Congress attempted to ferret out corruption in political campaigns by restricting the ability of individuals to wield undue influence on the political process. However, a key controversy erupted as a result of these restrictions. Did the limits in question violate freedom of speech and association under the First Amendment of the Constitution? In a very complicated decision, the justices of the Supreme Court made two substantive conclusions through a *per curiam* opinion. First, the restrictions placed on individual contributions to political campaigns did not violate the First Amendment:

> It is unnecessary to look beyond the Act's primary purpose—to limit the actuality and appearance of corruption resulting from large individual financial contributions—in order to find a constitutionally sufficient justification for the $1,000 contribution limitation. Under a system of private financing of elections, a candidate lacking immense personal or family wealth must depend on financial contributions from others to provide the resources necessary to conduct a successful campaign. The increasing importance of the communications media and sophisticated mass-mailing and polling operations to effective campaigning make the raising of large sums of money an ever more essential ingredient of an effective candidacy. To the extent that large contributions are given to secure a political *quid pro quo* from current and potential office holders, the integrity of our system of representative democracy is undermined. Although the scope of such pernicious practices can never be reliably ascertained, the deeply disturbing examples surfacing after the 1972 election demonstrate that the problem is not an illusory one.[34]

Second, the justices determined that the governmental restriction of independent expenditures in campaigns, the limitation on expenditures by candidates from their own personal or family resources, and the limitation on total campaign expenditures did, in fact, violate the First Amendment. The judicial reasoning employed is that because the aforementioned practices do not necessarily enhance the potential for corruption that individual contributions to candidates do, restricting them did not serve a government interest significant enough to warrant a curtailment on free speech and association:

> In sum, the provisions of the Act that impose a $1,000 limitation on contributions to a single candidate, a $5,000 limitation on contributions by a political action committee to a single candidate, and a $25,000 limitation on total contributions by an individual during any calendar year, are constitutionally valid. These limitations, along with the disclosure provisions, constitute the Act's primary weapons against the reality or appearance of improper influence stemming from the dependence of candidates on large campaign contributions. The contribution ceilings thus serve the basic governmental interest in safeguarding the integrity of the electoral process without directly impinging upon the rights of individual citizens and candidates to engage in political debate and discussion. By contrast, the First Amendment requires the invalidation of the Act's independent expenditure ceiling, its limitation on a candidate's expenditures from his own personal funds, and its ceilings on over-all campaign expenditures. These provisions place substantial and direct restrictions on the ability of candidates, citizens, and associations to engage in protected political expression, restrictions that the First Amendment cannot tolerate.[35]

The justices also issued a few other rulings with regard to this case. Under the 1974 amendments, the original members of the Federal Election Commission were appointed by the president, the speaker of the House, and the president *pro tempore* of the Senate (each appointed two of the six commissioners). The justices determined that this provision violated the principle of separation of powers as four of the commissioners were appointed by Congress but exercised executive powers. Thus, Congress would need to change its manner of selecting the commissioners. In addition, the justices upheld the FECA provision that authorized new measures to promote public financing of presidential campaigns, such as the income tax check-off. The justices concluded that this part of the law did not violate the First Amendment because it furthered First Amendment values by using public monies to encourage political debate in society.

The decision in *Buckley v. Valeo* was announced on January 30, 1976, during a presidential election year.[36] Congress responded to the Court's decision later that same year by passing new amendments to the FECA that required that all six members of the Federal Election Commission be appointed by the president and confirmed by the Senate.[37] Shortly thereafter, party leaders asked members of Congress to make further adjustments to the law, and changes were made again in 1979.

FECA Amendments of 1979

Many political candidates and officials representing political committees believed that the disclosure requirements forced unnecessary and burdensome paperwork on them, which had the effect of increasing administrative costs in campaigns.[38] State and local party leaders maintained that the law reduced the overall level of spending for traditional party-building activities, such as voter registration drives and mobilization efforts, because party leaders were restricted in the amount they could spend on behalf of candidates. Thus, a number of changes were made in the law. The 1979 amendments reduced the maximum number of reports that committees had to file during an election cycle, increased the threshold amount for reportable contributions or expenditures from $100 to $200, and increased the threshold for disclosing independent expenditures from $100 to $250. These changes substantially decreased the amount of information that candidates and committees had to file with the FEC.[39]

Another important change was made in the law in order to enhance the role of political parties and elections and to encourage higher levels of political participation amongst the citizenry. The revised law exempted certain types of party-related activity from spending limitations, including grassroots volunteer activities and voter registration and turnout drives. Political committees could also spend unlimited amounts on materials related to grassroots or volunteer activities, provided that the funds in question were not drawn from contributions designated for a specific candidate.[40] These exemptions, or loopholes, have generally been referred to as soft money. The 1979 amendments to the FECA were the last major campaign finance reforms in the United States until the early 21st century.

Bipartisan Campaign Reform Act of 2002

The Bipartisan Campaign Reform Act (BCRA), otherwise known as McCain-Feingold, amended the FECA of 1971. Its chief sponsors were John McCain (R-Arizona) and Russell Feingold (D-Wisconsin) in the Senate and Christopher Shays (R-Connecticut) and Martin Meehan (D-Massachusetts) in the House. Advocates of campaign finance reform argued that the unprecedented activities during the 1996 presidential campaign rendered the FECA relatively meaningless and necessitated new changes in federal law. The increase in soft money contributions to both major political parties and the advent of candidate-specific issue advertising demonstrated to many that changes were essential or the prominence of money in federal political campaigns would only get worse. Within the context of separate investigations of party fund raising practices during this election by

Congress, the U.S. Department of Justice, and the FEC, reformers sought to make campaign finance reform a high priority on the congressional legislative agenda. Yet in the late 1990s, Senators McCain and Feingold did receive majority support in both houses for their bill but were thwarted in their reform effort by a filibuster in the Senate conducted by Mitch McConnell (R-Kentucky), a leading opponent to campaign finance reform in Congress.[41]

Advocates for reform, however, did not capitulate to their opponents when a new Congress convened in 2001 following the contentious, and protracted, presidential election of 2000. Soft money fund raising to the parties had increased from $262 million in 1996 to $495 million in 2000; a surge in issue advocacy advertising also occurred during this election. These realities strengthened the resolve of congressional reformers, but some other important factors at the time contributed to the successful passage of the BCRA. More supporters of campaign finance reform were elected in 2000. This facilitated passing the bill in the Senate in particular, but a favorable political climate for campaign finance reform was created by the scandal involving the Enron Corporation. Enron was a very large energy company, and questions about the influence of contributions made in the name of the corporation on legislative and administrative actions that benefited the company were widely debated in the popular media. Enron's chief officer, Kenneth Lay, was identified as a political supporter of George W. Bush, and a significant amount of media coverage was focused on the reality that both Democrats and Republicans had accepted contributions from a company where top leaders made a great deal of money before the company collapsed, while hundreds of workers lost their jobs and their retirement income simultaneously. This context provided an incentive for a bipartisan endorsement of reform. After extensive legislative negotiations and procedural wrangling, President George W. Bush signed the act into law on March 27, 2002.[42] Almost immediately, the constitutionality of the BCRA was challenged in court.

The BCRA banned soft money in federal elections. A national party committee, including any entity that may be directly or indirectly affiliated with it, may not solicit, receive, spend, or direct to another person a contribution, donation, or transfer of funds not subject to federal prohibitions, contribution limits, and disclosure requirements. The BCRA also prohibited nonpartisan "issue ads" funded by soft money from corporations and labor unions. Ads referring to candidates for federal election without expressly advocating their election or defeat were banned 60 days before a general election and 30 days prior to a primary election. The law also required the disclosure of sources of funding for "electioneering communications" in excess of $10,000 a year. Finally, the legal limits of hard money contributions by individuals were raised and indexed for inflation.[43] The law went into effect on November 6, 2002, one day after the midterm federal elections. The individual contribution limit was raised from $1,000 to $2,000 per candidate per election. Because the limits were indexed for inflation, individuals may contribute the following amounts during the 2009–10 election season:

$2,400 per candidate per election
$5,000 to a political action committee per year
$10,000 per year combined limit for state, district, and local party committees
$30,400 per year to a national party committee
$115,500 biennial limit
($45,600 to all candidates and $69,900 to all PACs and parties)[44]

McConnell v. Federal Election Commission (2003)

The Supreme Court justices reviewed a decision from a special three-judge panel consisting of two district court judges and a presiding circuit court judge. The appeal went directly to the Supreme Court under the BCRA. As the case was complicated, an unusually long four hours of oral argument was scheduled to consider the constitutional issues involved. Similar to *Buckley v. Valeo,* the justices were deeply divided depending upon the issue at hand. Two central questions had to be resolved by the justices of the High Court. First, did the ban on soft money in the BCRA exceed the authority of Congress to regulate elections under Article I, Section 4 and/or violate freedom of speech under the First Amendment? Second, do regulations of the source, content, or timing of political advertising under the BCRA violate freedom of speech under the First Amendment? For the most part, the justices answered both questions negatively, in a five-to-four decision written by Justices Sandra Day O'Connor and John Paul Stevens.[45]

Justices O'Connor and Stevens declared that:

Many years ago we observed that "[t]o say that Congress is without power to pass appropriate legislation to safeguard . . . an election from the improper use of money to influence the result is to deny to the nation in a vital particular the power of self protection." We abide by that conviction in considering Congress' most recent effort to confine the ill effects of aggregated wealth on our political system. We are under no illusion that BCRA will be the last congressional statement on the matter. Money, like water, will always find an outlet. What problems will arise, and how Congress will respond, are concerns for another day. In the main we uphold BCRA's two principal, complementary features: the control of soft money and the regulation of electioneering communications.[46]

The veteran justices are reflecting on more than a century of history that suggests that despite many attempts to regulate the flow of money in federal political campaigns, Congress will undoubtedly revisit the issue many more times in the foreseeable future.

SUMMARY

The flow of money in presidential and congressional campaigns has increased steadily with the passage of time. In spite of many attempts at campaign finance reform by Congress, millions and millions of U.S. dollars are raised and spent in order to elect presidents, senators, and members of the House. The status quo has changed very little since the days of Theodore Roosevelt. Many individuals and political committees are presumably competing for access to elected officials so that their views on public policy issues can be offered to power brokers in charge of making policy for the American people. The downside of this process is quite clear. Many Americans perceive that decision makers are not aware of, and are perhaps indifferent to, their plight in this world. In a diverse, democratic republic such as the United States, the high costs of federal campaigns have contributed to a general malaise amongst the people. Too many Americans subscribe to the elitist premise that public policy is, to a large extent, controlled by the rich and powerful. This reality is very difficult to measure but clearly has deep roots in U.S. political history.

Chapter 6

THE PATH TO ENHANCED DEMOCRACY: A BLUEPRINT FOR ELECTORAL REFORM IN THE UNITED STATES

Recently, there has been a renewed debate concerning the relevancy of the political science discipline in American politics and public policy. In particular, some political scientists maintain that, in an effort to be scientific, they should avoid public policy advocacy as it interferes with the scientific nature of their inquiry.[1] I do not believe, however, that being scientific and engaging in public policy advocacy are mutually exclusive. Assuming that the enterprise in question has met sufficient scientific requirements and criteria, political scientists have a responsibility to engage in policy advocacy because why should they avoid doing so when they collectively have a great deal of knowledge and experience to share with the general public? Not engaging in the public policy debates of our time is a disservice because they have much to offer. In no way am I suggesting that political scientists have all the answers to our policy challenges. Our trained political scientists have a responsibility to contribute to this complex network and should be expected to do so. The avoidance of such activities is an abrogation of professional duties and is demonstrative of poor citizenship. In short, political scientists can and must set a better example given our collective commitment to the pursuit and imparting of knowledge. After all, many political scientists are assisting in the training of future leaders. If we expect students to get engaged in the American democracy, we should probably do so ourselves lest we be criticized, and rightfully so, for practicing hypocrisy.

THE IMPORTANCE OF THEORY IN AMERICAN POLITICS AND POLICY

It should be noted at this time that the most important aspect of politics, and this oftentimes is ignored due to the tendency of many to focus on, *inter alia,* conflict, scandal, polling, and money, is theory. Plausible theory is essential in the pursuit of more scientific knowledge about given political phenomena. As the prodigious student of law Oliver Wendell Holmes, Jr., echoed a long time ago:

> Theory is the most important part of the dogma of the law, as the architect is the most important man who takes part if the building of a house. The most important improvements in the last twenty-five years are improvements in theory. It is not to be feared as unpractical, for, to the competent, it simply means going to the bottom of the subject. For the incompetent, it sometimes is true, as has been said, that an interest in general ideas means an absence of particular knowledge. I remember in army days reading of a youth who, being examined for the lowest grade and being asked a question about squadron drill, answered that he never had considered the evolutions of less than ten thousand men. But the weak and foolish must be left to their folly. The danger is that the able and practical minded should look with indifference or distrust upon ideas the connection of which with their business is remote.[2]

As Justice Holmes indicated, people tend to equate money with success and power. In other words, wealthy individuals must be intelligent or they would not find themselves in such a privileged position in society. To this, he provides an unequivocal response:

> To an imagination of any scope the most far-reaching form of power is not money, it is the command of ideas. If you want great examples, read Mr. Leslie Stephen's *History of English Thought in the Eighteenth Century,* and see how a hundred years after his death the abstract speculations of Descartes had become a practical force controlling the conduct of men. Read the works of the great German jurists, and see how much more the world is governed today by Kant than by Bonaparte. We cannot all be Descartes or Kant, but we all want happiness. And happiness, I am sure from having known many successful men, cannot be won simply by being counsel for great corporations and having an income of fifty thousand dollars. An intellect great enough to win the prize needs other food besides success. The remoter and more general aspects of the law are those which give it universal interest. It is through them that you not only become a great master in your calling, but connect your subject with the universe and catch an echo of the infinite, a glimpse of its unfathomable process, a hint of the universal law.[3]

When Justice Holmes gave this speech to aspiring attorneys in 1897,[4] he was an associate justice of the Massachusetts Supreme Judicial Court. He would later be the Chief Justice on that court (1899–1902) and then an associate justice of the U.S. Supreme Court (1902–1932). What he is saying about the law is equally applicable to politics. The solution to the challenges that exist with regard to elections is theoretical in nature. In other words, if the status quo can be enhanced, and if the electoral process can be made more democratic, then the solution to America's electoral challenges can be found by concocting ideas that are reasonable, intuitive, and perhaps just downright common sense. It is with this spirit and a keen appreciation of history that I will offer some democratic reforms that, if implemented, would reflect more favorably on the American republic than is presently the case. In no way, however, is there even a hint that the reforms in question will somehow result in a utopian world. I simply contend that the implementation of the changes offered would continue America's long trek toward a more democratic nation state, something that is deeply entrenched in its evolving history.

THE IMPORTANCE OF STUDYING HISTORY IN AMERICAN POLITICS AND POLICY

Before proceeding, it is important to emphasize the study of history in any venue. Certainly this is crucial in the sector of American politics and public policy, as oftentimes contemporary citizens perceive that certain challenges are somehow novel and unique to them. While technology is ever changing, many of our political, ideological, partisan, and policy debates have been around for a long time. The political actors may change, but the issues remain fairly constant, and much can be learned from the successes, and the mistakes, of the past. When ascertaining the importance of history to legal studies, Justice Holmes reasoned that:

> At present, in very many cases, if we want to know why a rule of law has taken its particular shape, and more or less if we want to know why it exists at all, we go to tradition. We follow it into the Year Books, and perhaps beyond them to the customs of the Salian Franks, and somewhere in the past, in the German forests, in the needs of the Norman kings, in the assumptions of a dominant class, in the absence of generalized ideas, we find out the practical motive for what now best is justified by the mere fact of its acceptance and that men are accustomed to it. The rational study of law is still to a large extent the study of history. History must be a part of the study, because without it we cannot know the precise scope of rules which it is our business to know. It is a part of the rational study, because it is a first step toward an

enlightened skepticism, that is, towards a deliberate reconsideration of the worth of those rules. When you get the dragon out of his cave on to the plain and in the daylight, you can count his teeth and claws, and see just what is his strength. But to get him out is only the first step. The next is either to kill him, or to tame him and make him a useful animal. For the rational study of the law the blackletter man may be the man of the present, but the man of the future is the man of statistics and the master of economics. It is revolting to have no better reason for a rule of law than that so it was laid down in the time of Henry IV. It is still more revolting if the grounds upon which it was laid down have vanished long since, and the rule simply persists from blind imitation of the past.[5]

It seems to me that election laws and policies that do not serve a reasonable purpose and are reflective of past attitudes, beliefs, and perhaps even unfairness toward some citizens are ripe for reconsideration. In the public policy process, laws, even prudent ones that serve the greater public good, require constant revision. Even the Constitution, the supreme law of the land in the American federal republic, can be changed.

AMENDING THE FEDERAL CONSTITUTION

The reader will recall that the Framers themselves created formal mechanisms for amending the Constitution because they presumably understood the reality that all human beings are fallible and thus capable of erring at any time. After all, some of the Framers had previously signed the Articles of Confederation and Perpetual Union, and America's first experiment in democratic governance failed in a short period of time.[6] The constitutional amendment process is the essence of Article V of the U.S. Constitution:

> The Congress, whenever two thirds of both Houses shall deem it necessary, shall propose Amendments to this Constitution, or, on the Application of the Legislatures of two thirds of the several States, shall call a Convention for proposing Amendments, which, in either Case, shall be valid to all Intents and Purposes, as part of this Constitution, when ratified by the Legislatures of three fourths of the several States, or by Conventions in three fourths thereof, as the one or the other Mode of Ratification may be proposed by the Congress; Provided that no Amendment which may be made prior to the Year One thousand Eight hundred and eight shall in any Manner affect the first and fourth Clauses in the Ninth Section of the first Article; and that no State, without its Consent, shall be deprived of its equal Suffrage in the Senate.

For amendment proposals, the procedure of allowing two-thirds of the state legislatures to ask members of Congress to call a national convention has never been used. In terms of ratifying amendments, all but one amendment has been ratified in the same manner—by three-fourths of the state legislatures. Only the Twenty-First Amendment, which repealed Prohibition, was ratified by conventions in three-fourths of the states as opposed to the legislative bodies.

A WORD ABOUT THE ORIGINAL INTENT DEBATE

Because the Framers included procedures to alter the very document that they created, and because we know that James Madison himself did not support all aspects of the Constitution,[7] I do not accept the premise that the Constitution is a sacred document that can never be changed. If this were the case, then slavery would still exist and only a small percentage of the population could legally vote. Thus, I cannot endorse the theory of original intent, or originalism, as a viable approach to constitutional interpretation. If the Framers wanted future generations of Americans to either follow the original Constitution strictly, or the intent of Congress when the Constitution was amended, then why is the Constitution such a short statement and vague on many of the great issues of the day? Ascertaining the original intent of the Framers, in particular, is cumbersome and in many cases virtually impossible. The Bill of Rights was added to the Constitution two years after ratification (1791) largely due to the efforts of James Madison. What, exactly, did he and members of Congress mean, in all certainty and precision, with regard to the right to bear arms? It seems to me that advocates of both gun ownership rights as well as gun control have been arguing for years about this, and little has been resolved in a concrete manner. Are we to believe that if the Constitution is silent on a matter, then the issue or right in question does not exist? Do Americans only have the rights that are explicitly enumerated in the Constitution and nothing else?

   These fundamental questions are important because there are some who oppose changing the Constitution under any circumstances, even when they may not know much about the document. For example, the American Bar Association commissioned a national public opinion poll in 1991 that coincided with the 200th anniversary of the ratification of the Bill of Rights on December 15, 1791. In this poll, it was discovered that only 33 percent of American adults could correctly identify the Bill of Rights, and only 9 percent of the people knew that the Bill of Rights was adopted to protect them from abuses by the federal government.[8] I believe that it is important to understand that while the Framers of the Constitution were remarkable men in many ways and very successful with regard to the creation of a constitutional republic, they were human, and they did make mistakes not unlike all people during the evolution of human history.

The late Thurgood Marshall gave a speech in 1987 that was part of the bicentennial celebration of the drafting of the Constitution.[9] As politicians and federal judges around the nation were praising the Framers for their constitutional acumen, Justice Marshall was poignant in his criticism of the Framers for erring on many fronts. His remarks garnered a great deal of press coverage. He refutes the theory of original intent and instead argues that the Constitution is a "living document":

> I do not believe that the meaning of the Constitution was forever "fixed" at the Philadelphia Convention. Nor do I find the wisdom, foresight, and sense of justice exhibited by the Framers particularly profound. To the contrary, the government they devised was defective from the start, requiring several amendments, a civil war, and momentous social transformation to attain the system of constitutional government, and its respect for the individual freedoms and human rights, we hold as fundamental today. When contemporary Americans cite "The Constitution," they invoke a concept that is vastly different from what the Framers barely began to construct two centuries ago.[10]

To Marshall, contemporary citizens need to look no further than the first three words of the preamble to understand the Framers' perceptions of social justice:

> For a sense of the evolving nature of the Constitution we need look no further than the first three words of the document's preamble: "We the People." When the Founding Fathers used this phrase in 1787, they did not have in mind the majority of America's citizens. "We the People" included, in the words of the Framers, "the whole Number of free Persons." On a matter so basic as the right to vote, for example, Negro slaves were excluded, although they were counted for representational purposes at three fifths each. Women did not gain the right to vote for over a hundred and thirty years.
>
> These omissions were intentional. The record of the Framers' debates on the slave question is especially clear: The Southern States acceded to the demands of the New England States for giving Congress broad power to regulate commerce, in exchange for the right to continue the slave trade. The economic interests of the regions coalesced: New Englanders engaged in the "carrying trade" would profit from transporting slaves from Africa as well as goods produced in America by slave labor. The perpetuation of slavery ensured the primary source of wealth in the Southern states.[11]

Thus, to Justice Marshall, the most important aspect of the bicentennial of the drafting of the Constitution is not blind reverence for what happened long ago but celebrating what has happened since 1787 in the United States:

And so we must be careful, when focusing on the events which took place in Philadelphia two centuries ago, that we not overlook the momentous events which followed, and thereby lose our proper sense of perspective. Otherwise, the odds are that for many Americans the bicentennial celebration will be little more than a blind pilgrimage to the shrine of the original document now stored in a vault in the National Archives. If we seek, instead, a sensitive understanding of the Constitution's inherent defects, and its promising evolution through 200 years of history, the celebration of the "Miracle at Philadelphia" will, in my view, be a far more meaningful and humbling experience. We will see that the true miracle was not the birth of the Constitution, but its life, a life nurtured through two turbulent centuries of our own making, and a life embodying much good fortune that was not.

Thus, in this bicentennial year, we may not all participate in the festivities with flagwaving fervor. Some may more quietly commemorate the suffering, struggle, and sacrifice that has triumphed over much of what was wrong with the original document, and observe the anniversary with hopes not realized and promises not filled. I plan to celebrate the bicentennial of the Constitution as a living document, including the Bill of Rights and the other amendments protecting individual freedoms and human rights.[12]

The late Justice Marshall articulated his belief in the theory of the Constitution as a living document. To him, the Constitution was intended to be a base foundation to apply to an ever-changing society. Inherent in this theory is a premise that the Constitution is not static and rigid but flexible and dynamic and, therefore, adaptable to a vibrant republic where civil liberties will continually expand and where democracy will flourish over time.[13]

THE CONSTITUTION AS A "LIVING DOCUMENT"—THE NOTION OF ACTIVE LIBERTY

Justice Stephen Breyer articulated his judicial philosophy in a book published in 2005.[14] His primary contention is that constitutional interpretation should be guided by active liberty, or the ability of the people to share in governance by being allowed to make public policy. Democratic participation is the essence of active liberty; to him, democratic participation is the true spirit embodied in the U.S. Constitution. As Justice Breyer articulated: "The United States is a nation built upon principles of liberty. That liberty means not only freedom from government coercion but also the freedom to participate in the government itself."[15] Many scholars believe that Justice Breyer's book is a direct refutation of another book published earlier by one of his colleagues on the Court, Justice Antonin Scalia.[16]

Justice Scalia delineated his judicial philosophy in a 1997 book where he contends that judges should rely on a the literal text of the Constitution or statute and ascertain the original meaning of the Framers, or Congress with regard to the amendments, when deciding cases. To him, this approach limits judicial policy making and prevents judges from being overly subjective in their decision making.[17] But Justice Breyer refutes originalism, oftentimes referred to as textualism or strict constructionism, as a fundamentally flawed jurisprudence touted by self-professed conservatives. Adherents to originalism participate in a process that commonly results in an undemocratic outcome. Yet in advance of scrutinizing the plausibility of specific case outcomes and the legal rules established in various cases, Justice Breyer questions the very nature of the originalist approach to judicial decision-making:

> The answer, in my view, lies in the unsatisfactory nature of their approach. First, the more "originalist" judges cannot appeal to the Framers themselves in support of their interpretive views. The Framers did not say specifically what factors judges should take into account when they interpret statutes or the Constitution . . . Why would the Framers, who disagreed even about the necessity of *including* a Bill of Rights in the Constitution, who disagreed about the *content* of that Bill of Rights, nonetheless have agreed about *what school of interpretive thought* should prove dominant in interpreting that Bill of Rights in the centuries to come?[18]

A fixed viewpoint about rights in general can produce an unfortunate result that runs counter to the constitutional spirit espoused by the Framers in the grand convention.

Justice Breyer is basically offering a utilitarian case for a judicial decision-making process that results in implementing the democratic intentions embodied in the U.S. Constitution (the Framers and Congress alike with the amendments). This judicial philosophy has a rather lengthy tradition in American jurisprudence. In the celebrated case involving the national bank controversy in the early 19th century (*McCulloch v. Maryland*),[19] Congress had chartered the Bank of the United States on two occasions (1791 and 1816). The First Bank of the United States was established at the urging of Secretary of Treasury Alexander Hamilton. It folded in 1811 due to a lack of congressional support. However, the high inflation that ensued after the War of 1812 compelled members of Congress to establish the Second Bank of the United States. Soon thereafter, the constitutionality of the bank was challenged by Maryland state officials.[20]

The members of the Maryland state legislature passed a law that effectively taxed all banks operating within the state that were not chartered by the state. Only one such bank existed: the Baltimore branch of the Bank of the United States. When the cashier of the Baltimore branch was approached to pay the state tax, he declined. Maryland officials took their case to state court.[21]

A primary contention between the two sides, officials representing both the national government and the Maryland state government, had to do with constitutional interpretation. From the perspective of federal officials, Congress created the Bank of the United States in pursuance of its constitutional powers. Specifically, the last section (paragraph 18) of Article I, Section 8 provides the following: "To make all Laws which shall be necessary and proper for carrying into Execution the foregoing Powers, and all other Powers vested by this Constitution in the Government of the United States, or in any Department or Officer thereof."

Maryland state officials believed the Bank of the United States to be unconstitutional because the Framers did not explicitly include this authority in the enumerated powers of Congress. As representatives of a sovereign state, the legislators had the authority to tax the Bank of the United States because federal power emanated from the states and not the people. Chief Justice John Marshall penned the opinion in *McCulloch*,[22] and he refuted the states' rights arguments of Maryland officials:

> the counsel for the state of Maryland have deemed it of some importance, in the construction of the constitution, to consider that instrument, not as emanating from the people, but as the act of sovereign and independent states. The powers of the general government, it has been said, are delegated by the states, who alone are truly sovereign; and must be exercised in subordination to the states, who alone possess supreme dominion. It would be difficult to sustain this proposition. The convention which framed the constitution was indeed elected by the state legislatures. But the instrument, when it came from their hands, was a mere proposal, without obligation, or pretensions to it. It was reported to the then existing congress of the United States, with a request that it might be submitted to a convention of delegates, chosen in each state by the people thereof, under the recommendation of its legislature, for their assent and ratification. This mode of proceeding was adopted; and by the convention, by congress, and by the state legislatures, the instrument was submitted to the people. They acted upon it in the only manner in which they can act safely, effectively and wisely, on such a subject, by assembling in convention. It is true, they assembled in their several states—and where else should they have assembled? No political dreamer was ever wild enough to think of breaking down the lines which separate the states, and of compounding the American people into one common mass. Of consequence, when they act, they act in their states. But the measures they adopt do not, on that account, cease to be measures of the people themselves, or become the measures of the state governments.[23]

Chief Justice Marshall did not endorse a strict or narrow interpretation of the Constitution. Just because the word "bank" did not get incorporated into Article I, Section 8 did not mean that Congress was not authorized, under the Constitution, to create a national banking system. In his own words, the great Chief Justice offered the following judicial reasoning:

> Among the enumerated powers, we do not find that of establishing a bank or creating a corporation. But there is no phrase in the instrument which, like the articles of confederation, excludes incidental or implied powers; and which requires that everything granted shall be expressly and minutely described. Even the 10th amendment, which was framed for the purpose of quieting the excessive jealousies which had been excited, omits the word 'expressly,' and declares only, that the powers 'not delegated to the United States, nor prohibited to the states, are reserved to the states or to the people;' thus leaving the question, whether the particular power which may become the subject of contest, has been delegated to the one government, or prohibited to the other, to depend on a fair construction of the whole instrument. The man who drew and adopted this amendment had experienced the embarrassments resulting from the insertion of this word in the articles of confederation, and probably omitted it, to avoid those embarrassments. A constitution, to contain an accurate detail of all the subdivisions of which its great powers will admit, and of all the means by which they may be carried into execution, would partake of the prolixity of a legal code, and could scarcely be embraced by the human mind. It would, probably, never be understood by the public. Its nature, therefore, requires, that only its great outlines should be marked, its important objects designated, and the minor ingredients which compose those objects, be deduced from the nature of the objects themselves. That this idea was entertained by the framers of the American constitution, is not only to be inferred from the nature of the instrument, but from the language. Why else were some of the limitations, found in the 9th section of the 1st article, introduced? It is also, in some degree, warranted, by their having omitted to use any restrictive term which might prevent its receiving a fair and just interpretation. In considering this question, then, we must never forget that it is a constitution we are expounding.[24]

The chief justice provided a key substantive reality about constitutions— they are generally broad and somewhat vague by definition. A stable constitution is not one that is overly specific in nature but one that is flexible and provides foundational values and principles for future generations. Innate human behavior suggests that no one generation of peers has all the substantive answers to all policy challenges of future societies. Thus, a prudent approach to constitutional interpretation would be to embrace the Marshall viewpoint and not be too narrow in scope.

The essence of the *McCulloch* ruling is presented in a succinct manner by Chief Justice Marshall:

We admit, as all must admit, that the powers of the government are limited, and that its limits are not to be transcended. But we think the sound
construction of the constitution must allow to the national legislature that
discretion, with respect to the means by which the powers it confers are
to be carried into execution, which will enable that body to perform the
high duties assigned to it, in the manner most beneficial to the people. Let
the end be legitimate, let it be within the scope of the constitution, and all
means which are appropriate, which are plainly adopted to that end, which
are not prohibited, but consist with the letter and spirit of the constitution,
are constitutional.[25]

This type of philosophy with regard to constitutional interpretation is
clearly a reflection of Chief Justice Marshall's experience and world view.
He had witnessed the young country almost succumb to chaos twice—
during the Revolutionary War and during the War of 1812. From his perspective, it was a rigid adherence to a narrow interpretation of the Constitution and a states' rights doctrine that almost led to defeat in the struggle
for independence and again when the British invaded the Capitol a few
years before the *McCulloch* decision.

ACTIVE LIBERTY IN PRACTICE

Justice Breyer applies his judicial philosophy to six pragmatic applications,
including issues involving freedom of speech, federalism, privacy, affirmative action, statutory interpretation, and administrative law.[26] In each
scenario, he advocates a balance between the preservation of individual
civil liberties and promotion of the greater public good. An examination of
each issue suggests that his approach is similar in nature to the one taken
by Chief Justice John Marshall in the early 19th century and Justice Oliver
Wendell Holmes in the early 20th century.

Freedom of Speech

Freedom of speech and expression are essential components of any democratic society; in fact, the sheer essence of any democracy necessitates an
open exchange of ideas and opinions. Students of American history need
only to reflect upon the Alien and Sedition Acts of 1798 to appreciate this
fundamental reality.[27] The Federalist-controlled Congress passed four laws,
and President John Adams signed them into law. These acts, *inter alia,* restricted speech that was critical of the government and were designed to
silence and weaken Thomas Jefferson's opposition party (the Democratic-
Republicans). They were obviously an affront to the First Amendment and
contributed to the demise of the Federalist party in the 1800 elections.[28]

In a society where some have an absolutist position on civil liberties issues, Justice Breyer argues that:

> in applying First Amendment presumptions, we must distinguish among areas, contexts, and forms of speech. Reference to basic constitutional purposes can help generate the relevant distinctions. And reference back to at least one general purpose, active liberty, helps both to generate proper distinctions and also properly to apply the distinctions generated. The active liberty reference helps us to preserve speech that is essential to our democratic form of government, while simultaneously permitting the law to deal effectively with such modern regulatory problems as campaign finance and product or workplace safety.[29]

Thus, balancing constitutionally protected speech while allowing members of Congress sufficient authority to regulate the flow of money in elections and promote safety for workers, along with consumer protection measures, are not mutually exclusive endeavors.

Federalism

Americans have always debated differing conceptions of federalism throughout their history under the present Constitution. The appropriate sphere of policy-making power (national, state, and/or local levels of government) has been a source of controversy at least since the debate over ratification of the Constitution between the Federalists and the Anti-Federalists.[30] As the Framers stipulated in the supremacy clause of the Constitution:

> This Constitution, and the Laws of the United States which shall be made in Pursuance thereof; and all Treaties made, or which shall be made, under the Authority of the United States, shall be the supreme Law of the Land; and the Judges in every State shall be bound thereby, any Thing in the Constitution or Laws of any State to the Contrary notwithstanding.

Regardless of differing conceptions of federalism, clearly the Framers deemed it necessary, even essential, for the federal Constitution and federal laws to supersede state constitutions and statutes. In the American federal republic, the national government and the state governments are not equal; the superior status dedicated to the national government is undoubtedly due in part to the experience rendered under the Articles of Confederation and Perpetual Union.[31]

Justice Breyer offered his conception of a modern notion of federalism:

> In one sense, the Constitution's federal structure helps to protect modern liberty. A division of powers among federal and state governments makes it

more difficult for the federal government to tell state and local governments what to do. And it thereby frees citizens from restraints that a more distant central government might otherwise impose.[32]

Note that this vision of federalism does not result in the creation of a rubric that elucidates which level of government is best suited to address a plethora of public policy issues. Such ideological debates will persist as they are deeply rooted in theory and, therefore, cannot be resolved to the satisfaction of all citizens by definition.

Privacy

The right to privacy was first mentioned in American jurisprudence in an important article published in *Harvard Law Review* in 1890 by Samuel Warren and Louis Brandeis, two partners in a Boston law firm.[33] Twenty-six years later Louis Brandeis was appointed by President Woodrow Wilson to the U.S. Supreme Court, and he was confirmed by the U.S. Senate, becoming the first Jewish American to serve on the High Court.[34] In their article, the attorneys provided a basic conception for the right to privacy, a right that is not explicitly mentioned in the U.S. Constitution but one that is implied by the sheer existence of other constitutional safeguards:

> That the individual shall have full protection in person and in property is a principle as old as the common law; but it has been found necessary from time to time to define anew the exact nature and extent of such protection. Political, social, and economic changes entail the recognition of new rights, and the common law, in its eternal youth, grows to meet the demands of society. Thus, in very early times, the law gave a remedy only for physical interference with life and property, for trespasses *vi et armis*. Then the "right to life" served only to protect the subject from battery in its various forms; liberty meant freedom from actual restraint; and the right to property secured to the individual his lands and his cattle. Later, there came a recognition of man's spiritual nature, of his feelings and his intellect. Gradually the scope of these legal rights broadened; and now the right to life has come to mean the right to enjoy life,—the right to be let alone; the right to liberty secures the exercise of extensive civil privileges; and the term "property" has grown to comprise every form of possession—intangible, as well as tangible.[35]

The quintessential conception of the right to privacy, as noted by the Boston lawyers before the turn of the 20th century, is the right simply to be left alone. A strict or narrow interpretation of the Constitution would not corroborate such a doctrine. Yet who would dispute the contention that democratic citizens have freedom from government intrusion so long as they do not break the laws of the state or infringe upon the rights of their fellow citizens?

In analyzing the right to privacy, Justice Breyer declared that:

> The privacy example suggests more, in respect to judicial caution. It warns against adopting an overly rigid method of interpreting the Constitution— placing weight upon eighteenth-century details to the point at which it becomes difficult for a twenty-first century court to apply the document's underlying values.[36]

Federal judges have to embrace the reality that their approach to decision making has real world consequences and public policy implications. Technological advances are presumably part of the human condition. They will continue, undoubtedly, as clever minds concoct ways to improve the daily lives of citizens. Thus, a rigid orthodoxy when it comes to interpreting the Constitution has some profound realities associated with the practice. In short, it will likely curtail civil liberties in the world's oldest democracy, an outcome that few would endorse regardless of ideological inclination.

Affirmative Action

Federal affirmative action programs were created in the 1960s to enhance diversity in the workforce and in higher education programs. The fundamental premise of affirmative action is to provide equality of opportunity, particularly to women and people of color, in securing employment and gaining promotions on the job as well as gaining access to professional fields that require various levels of formal education. Historically, both groups were discriminated against by some Americans and so federal officials, led initially by President John F. Kennedy and then President Lyndon B. Johnson, determined that affirmative action programs were both justified and needed in American society.[37]

When the Supreme Court justices were asked to review the constitutionality of affirmative action programs 25 years apart,[38] the justices had to scrutinize the equal protection clause of the Fourteenth Amendment. In so doing, Justice Breyer echoed the collective mind set of the Court's majority in both instances: "When faced with one interpretation of the Equal Protection Clause that, through efforts to include, would facilitate the functioning of democracy and a different interpretation of the Equal Protection Clause that, through perceived exclusion, might impede the functioning of our democracy, is it surprising that the Court majority chose the former?"[39] Again, Justice Breyer is emphasizing his premise that the justices on the Supreme Court, though appointed for lifetime terms, must not succumb to originalism, particularly in the case of affirmative action, as opposing its constitutionality would have the effect of contradicting the democratic principles embodied in the Constitution and promoting racial strife and divide in the nation.

Statutory Interpretation

Justice Breyer contends that an overemphasis on the text of a statute can lead federal judges astray and compel them to divorce law from life and, in so doing, results in the creation of a new law that harms those whom members of Congress intended to help.[40] As a result, he concludes that when it comes to interpreting statutes passed by Congress or state legislatures:

> a 'reasonable legislator' approach is a workable method of implementing the Constitution's democratic objective. It permits ready translation of the general desire of the public for certain ends, through the legislator's efforts to embody those ends in legislation, into a set of statutory words that will carry out those general objectives.[41]

It is important to highlight the judicial standard of reasonableness when it comes to interpretation of the law. This is obviously not an exact standard, but law is not a precise science but a human-driven enterprise. It is incumbent upon federal judges to reasonably apply the intent of legislators when adjudicating disputes between two or more parties. Utilizing this common sense approach is predicated on the reality that there are policy consequences when court cases are decided by judges. Because this is the reality of judicial decision making, and always has been, the suggestion that judges should rely on originalism and somehow as a result avoid judicial policy making is a subterfuge and does not reflect the applied world of politics and public policy.

Administrative Law

Administrative law highlights an important dilemma in modern life, as Justice Breyer articulated:

> The average citizen normally lacks the time, knowledge, and experience necessary to understand certain technical matters related, for example, to the environment, energy, communications, or modern weaponry. Without delegation to experts, an inexpert public, possessing the will, would lack the way. The public understands this fact. . . . The Framers foresaw this possibility. They sought to create a workable democracy—a democratic process capable of acting for the public good.[42]

A reasonable balance with regard to public administrators is essential in modern society. In a democracy, government officials must be ultimately accountable to the people. Administrators are people with technical expertise about their respective public policy fields. Thus, legislators can delegate some of their authority to administrators but not too much because there would be a deficiency with accountability issues. As Justice Breyer advocates, perhaps this delicate balance can best be achieved by the principle of judicial deference. A prominent case in administrative law, *Chevron U.S.A., Inc. v. Natural Resources Defense Council, Inc.*,[43] illustrates this principle in practice. The justices of the High Court determined that a judge should defer to a reasonable interpretation of an ambiguous statute by agency administrators. Such an approach not only seems concrete in pragmatic terms, but it also conforms to democratic principles that should never be compromised.

THE IMPORTANCE OF CONSTITUTIONAL INTERPRETATION

In a book on electoral reform, some may question the plausibility or even relevancy of incorporating a discussion of constitutional interpretation by way of conclusion. I believe that this discussion is essential in the U.S. political system in particular, where law is created in numerous forms.[44] In short, electoral reform will not ensue simply by enacting federal and/ or state legislation. Federal judges and how they interpret the Constitution and statutory law will continue to affect the electoral process in the United States. Public administrators, charged with the important task of the implementation of public policies, will assuredly do the same. Thus, a systemic approach to the issue at hand will presumably result in a more informed discourse and debate on the subject.

A BLUEPRINT FOR ELECTORAL REFORM

I do not presume to have all the answers when it comes to electoral reform. However, based on America's own democratic tradition, I believe that the following reform proposals would cumulatively contribute to enhancing democracy in the United States and would result in more responsive governance, something that clearly has been experienced throughout American history and is a great source of pride for many democrats and republicans alike.

Reform Proposal #1: Strengthen the Political Parties

The prominent political scientist, E. E. Schattschneider, defined democracy in the following manner: "Democracy is a competitive political system in which competing leaders and organizations define the alternatives of public policy in such a way that the public can participate in the decision-making process."[45] From his perspective, political parties and their officials are one of the leading facilitators of democracy in America because party leaders provide the masses with policy options, which in turn allows the general public to participate in the public policy process in a meaningful manner.

Many years earlier, during World War II, Professor Schattschneider boldly declared that:

> The rise of political parties is indubitably one of the principal distinguishing marks of modern government. The parties, in fact, have played a major role as makers of governments, more especially they have been the makers of democratic government. It should be stated flatly at the outset that this volume is devoted to the thesis that the political parties created democracy and that modern democracy is unthinkable save in terms of the parties. As a matter of fact, the condition of the parties is the best possible evidence of the nature of any regime. The most important distinction in modern political philosophy, the distinction between democracy and dictatorship, can be made best in terms of party politics. The parties are not therefore merely appendages of modern government; they are in the center of it and play a determinative and creative role in it.[46]

Though many Americans view political parties in the abstract as being corrupt, self-serving, and even inhibiting the political process, Professor Schattschneider's prophesy has profound implications in the real world of politics. Strong political parties perform a fundamental role in democratic political systems. Strong (not corrupt) parties present a public policy platform and a slate of candidates to the voters. The voters can subsequently endorse or reject the policies and candidates put forth by party leaders. When prosperity is perceived, there is more clarity on the part of the electorate in terms of rewarding the party in power with additional terms in office and/or punishing them during perceived policy failures by ousting the incumbents and affording another party an opportunity to govern in a majoritarian sense.

This sentiment about stronger, and therefore more accountable, parties was reiterated by the committee on political parties of the American Political Science Association in 1950.[47] The primary thesis of the authors of this report ought to resonate with the reader 60 years after it was issued:

> Historical and other factors have caused the American two-party system to operate as two loose associations of state and local organizations, with very little national machinery and very little national cohesion. As a result,

either major party, when in power, is ill-equipped to organize its members in the legislative and executive branches into a government held together and guided by the party program. Party responsibility at the polls thus tends to vanish. This is a very serious matter, for it affects the very heartbeat of American democracy. It also poses grave problems of domestic and foreign policy in an era when it is no longer safe for the nation to deal piecemeal with issues that can be disposed of only on the basis of coherent programs.[48]

In basic terms, there must be a discernible link between electoral outcomes and public policy making. The people must be able to understand the policy implications of electing a Democratic president, a Republican president, a Republican Congress, a Democratic Congress, or divided government. This causal relationship between electoral outcomes and policy making has largely disappeared over the last 60 years or more. This would help to explain why, *inter alia*, issues concerning the federal budget are so frustrating for contemporary Americans. When a budget surplus occurred during the second term of Bill Clinton's presidency, many did not know whether the president should get most of the credit or the Republican Congress. Conversely, the dramatic increase in the total national debt that has occurred since 2001 has left many wondering whether officials in either major political party are serious about balancing the budget in the early part of the 21st century. Clearly, party affiliation is still an important cue for voters in the United States. However, with candidate-centered campaigns and individual candidates trying to package themselves to the electorate, it is very difficult to discern, in many cases, distinct differences between and among the major political parties today. This is certainly a contributing factor to the rise in divided party government over the last four decades.[49]

The rise of candidate-centered campaigns has made the parties less responsive to citizens. This needs to change, which is certainly not an original thought on my part. In 1950, political scientists across the country contended that:

Party responsibility means the responsibility of both parties to the general public, as enforced in elections. Party responsibility to the public, enforced in elections, implies that there be more than one party, for the public can hold a party responsible only if it has a choice. As a means of achieving responsibility, the clarification of party policy also tends to keep public debate on a more realistic level, restraining the inclination of party spokesmen to make unsubstantiated statements and charges.[50]

The public debate about politics has to change in the United States. It is very easy to run a symbolic campaign with a great deal of mudslinging and very little substance in presidential and congressional campaigns. This is a disservice to citizens. There is far too much emphasis on alleged character and patriotism issues and an insufficient focus on public policy ideas to improve the status quo.[51] Ultimately, campaigns should be all about the communication of different policy ideas to the citizenry. Name-calling needs to cease; we do not like to hear our children engage in this practice, and we should embrace the same common sense approach in the electoral arena.

One way to promote more responsible political parties is to ensure that all states have closed primaries. Currently, half of the states have some semblance of a closed primary, where only the voters who are registered with a party can vote in its primary; the remaining states have some version of an open primary, where voters of any party affiliation can vote for the slate of any party.[52] How this may be accomplished will be discussed later in the chapter. By the way, primary elections are not held in most democracies. Other democratic nations rely on a paradigm that prevailed in the United States throughout the 19th century: political party leaders will draft a platform and present a slate of candidates to the electorate. Citizens then have the opportunity to vote up or down. Yet the Progressives changed this approach with the advent of direct primaries. Limiting the primaries to registered members (all states would have to allow only partisan adherents the opportunity to participate) would enhance party discipline in the United States and provide more clarity to the voters. This should prove beneficial if citizens will also embrace reform. In order to hold party leaders and members more accountable, citizens absolutely must make politics more of a priority. In other words, as a collective entity, Americans need to educate themselves about current events and current leaders; in short, we need to increase our collective knowledge about politics. A more interested and informed citizen will be better positioned to demand more substantive campaigns and be less vulnerable to manipulative and nonsubstantive political campaigns. There is no question that the American political system is in need of reform. Democracy does not function well with a passive citizenry. If we wish to improve the manner in which government functions, it will not magically happen without extensive citizen involvement. Collectively, the people can and must be willing to become more engaged in this democratic republic. Such a noble enterprise is crucial to any reform scenario.

The reader may be thinking that changing the structure of primaries will not necessarily make parties more responsible to the electorate. I agree with this premise. Gimmickry and false bravado will not result in much by way of reform. There is a significant burden of proof on citizens, and systemic reform is required. It will only occur through enhanced education. There is no other way. Sound bites and chicanery will be wholly insufficient. There is not enough emphasis on American government in our decentralized K–12 public education system. Young people need more basic knowledge about American politics and public policy. Such knowledge is essential to becoming more proactive citizens. If we are frustrated about the inability of our leaders to address our policy challenges, then why not do something about this reality? Passivity and reticence will not result in any substantial and longitudinal reform.

It is particularly crucial for senior high school students to not only have a course in U.S. history, but American government as well. We have to provide fundamental knowledge necessary for democratic citizenship. A course in basic American national government and/or public affairs is essential at the baccalaureate level as well. Such a paradigmatic shift will take some time as many governmental levels and entities would be affected. Our collective willingness to become more educated and engaged will be judged by history and will impact future generations in a profound manner, hopefully for the better.

By the way, some of the other reform proposals that are offered in this chapter will transcend this issue. Some of the proposals, if enacted, would have a compounding effect on the political system in a way that is immeasurable in a quantitative manner at this point in time.

Reform Proposal #2: Reinvigorate Cooperative Federalism

The first two political parties emerged in the United States primarily due to ideological differences concerning the proper role of the federal government in society. Advocates of a national government with expansive policy powers believed that the path to prosperity was predicated upon assigning more legal authority to Congress and presumably less policy-making power to the state governments. Adherents to the states' rights ideology believed that Congress had a very limited mandate under the Constitution and all other powers and duties were left to the states. Yet the history of the nation has been fairly replete on the matter of states' rights—in order to promote more fairness and egalitarianism, the members of Congress at times have had to intervene and compel some of the states to alter their policies accordingly. Such a strategy is a constitutional prerogative of Congress under the supremacy clause. In the political arena historically, many members of Congress have sought to preserve their conception of the doctrine of states' rights. It seems to me that viable state policies should remain intact. There is a great deal of diversity in the American republic, and state officials should have the leeway to promote the greater public good in their respective jurisdictions. Having said that, in an unequivocal manner, the time for rigid orthodoxy when it comes to views of federalism is long past due. A role for the state governments in public policy making is guaranteed and protected in the U.S. Constitution. Yet, it is a subordinate role. When state officials create plausible and equitable policies for their citizens, national intrusion is not warranted. But when state officials have either not afforded their citizens constitutional guarantees and/or failed to create viable public policies, then Congress has a responsibility to intervene on behalf of the people involved.

This sentiment was echoed by a young mayor of Minneapolis, Minnesota, in 1948 when pondering the status of civil rights in America:

> My friends, to those who say that we are rushing this issue of civil rights, I say to them we are 172 years late. To those who say that this civil rights program is an infringement on states' rights, I say this: The time has arrived in America for the Democratic Party to get out of the shadow of states' rights and to walk forthrightly into the bright sunshine of human rights. People—human beings—this is the issue of the twentieth century. People of all kinds—all sorts of people—and these people are looking to America for leadership, and they're looking to America for precept and example.[53]

Hubert Humphrey subsequently made the following plea, which is still quite relevant today though it was made over 60 years ago:

> Let us do forget the evil passions and the blindness of the past. In these times of world economic, political, and spiritual—above all spiritual crises, we cannot and we must not turn from the path so plainly before us. The path has already lead us through many valleys of the shadow of death. And now is the time to recall those who were left on that path of American freedom.[54]

It is clear from the discussion included in Chapter 2 that some states have election laws that are lacking in comparative democratic terms. The time is past due for electoral reform, and it is incumbent upon Congress to intervene in conformance with the model of cooperative federalism of the past.[55]

The notion of cooperative federalism, dating back to the New Deal of the 1930s, is a recognition that all levels of government (local, state, and national) need to collaborate in order to address the needs of the people in an optimum manner. This approach to federalism supplanted a dominant belief system that prevailed in the United States for much of its history—the doctrine of dual federalism. This rigid doctrine was predicated on a belief that all powers not expressly granted to the national government were reserved for the states and the people. Unfortunately, this conception of federalism resulted in significant misfortune during the Great Depression of the 1920s and 1930s.[56]

Regardless of one's perception on how much power the national government should appropriately wield vis-à-vis state governments, it is important to heed the wisdom of both Alexander Hamilton and James Madison when they drafted *The Federalist Papers* after the Constitution was drafted in 1787.[57] Though they would later part ways politically, both reiterated a fundamental premise inherent in a republican form of government. Regardless of which level of government is charged with addressing specific policy issues, the ultimate sovereigns in the United States are the people, and government in a general sense is a mere trustee of the people. In *Federalist* No. 28, Mr. Hamilton noted that:

> Power being almost always the rival of power, the general government will at all times stand ready to check the usurpations of the state governments, and these will have the same disposition towards the general government. The people, by throwing themselves into either scale, will infallibly make it preponderate. If their rights are invaded by either, they can make use of the other as the instrument of redress. How wise will it be in them by cherishing the union to preserve to themselves an advantage which can never be too highly prized![58]

Mr. Madison made the following declaration in *Federalist* No. 46:

> I proceed to inquire whether the federal government or the State governments will have the advantage with regard to the prediction and support of the people. Notwithstanding the different modes in which they are appointed, we must consider both of them as substantially dependent on the great body of the citizens of the United States. I assume this position here as it respects the first, reserving the proofs for another place. The federal and State governments are in fact but different agents and trustees of the people, constituted with different powers, and designed for different purposes. The adversaries of the Constitution seem to have lost sight of the people altogether in their reasonings on this subject; and to have viewed these different establishments, not only as mutual rivals and enemies, but as uncontrolled by any common superior in their efforts to usurp the authorities of each other. These gentlemen must here be reminded of their error. They must be told that the ultimate authority, wherever the derivative may be found, resides in the people alone, and that it will not depend merely on the comparative ambition or address of the different governments, whether either, or which of them, will be able to enlarge its sphere of jurisdiction at the expense of the other.[59]

Perhaps it would be prudent in the early 21st century to focus less on conflicts over federalism and more on enhancing democracy and attending to the collective interests of the people. Making the American democracy more effective should be the primary focus; far less time and energy should be allocated to superfluous issues that are truly not that significant in substantive terms.

In order to reform American elections and to promote the cause of democracy in the United States, there are several reforms that should be enacted (review Chapter 2 by way of background). First, all of the states should do one of two things with regard to voter registration. The optimum scenario would be to replicate the North Dakota model, where all citizens become eligible to vote when they reach their 18th birthday. The potential electorate would be broadened considerably in the United States if all residents become theoretically eligible to vote when they became 18. Instead, we rely on voluntary registration, which excludes millions from voting in practical terms. A second option would be to have all states implement same-day registration based on the model established by Idaho, Iowa, Maine, Minnesota, Montana, New Hampshire, Wisconsin, and Wyoming. Although this approach would still rely on voluntary registration, it would at least make citizens eligible to vote on election day if they so desired. The precedent established in *Dunn v. Blumstein* has long outlived its utility. A 30-day waiting period for registration in advance of election day is not reasonable in today's terms. It is a mechanism of exclusion, which has a most unfortunate past in American history. Computer technology is far too sophisticated in the 21st century to substantively justify a waiting period of up to 30 days before an election. There is simply no justification for such laws, and they need to be eradicated without delay.

Voting is a preeminent right in a democracy. As such, citizens of the United States should be treated in an undifferentiated manner. The intrinsic value of all citizens is the same. Therefore, election laws should encourage participation as much as is practicable and should be expansive in nature. Because election day in early November is fairly institutionalized by this time in American history, it should remain intact, but early voting, which could manifest itself in many ways (e.g., the Oregon model with voting by mail elections), should be afforded to all citizens on the same basis. Traditional voting times should be more equitable as well. Allowing 15 hours[60] for voting on election day is a reasonable amount of time by contemporary standards to invest in democracy (e.g., the New York model). Closing the polls early (6 P.M.) sends an unfortunate message to citizens. It is time to revamp such statutes.

Similarly, the wide disparity of laws governing convicted felons and voting has to be revisited. Uniformity is needed because the United States is a nation of people first and foremost and not states. At the very least, convicted felons should have their voting rights restored upon the completion of their debt to society for their crimes. Permanent disenfranchisement for those who have completed their sentences is not justifiable. Arguably, such a policy has a disparate impact on specific groups in society (i.e., African Americans) and should not be tolerated.

In the absence of fraudulent voting, stringent identification laws that pose a disparate impact on the poor, racial minorities, and older Americans ought to be abolished as well. A clear and unequivocal message should be forwarded to the citizenry by its governing structures—the destiny of our democratic republic is in the hands of the people.

The diversity that exists in the American republic is clearly evidenced in Tables 2.8 and 2.9. The preservation of cultural traditions is an important and noteworthy endeavor. Yet, when it comes to voting and elections, all Americans should be on the same plane. Citizens in Maine, New York, Indiana, Colorado, Florida, and everywhere else should be treated in the same manner, and the world's oldest republic should establish a democratic model for other nations to emulate. Some states have invited and perhaps even encouraged national intervention because their laws do not promote participation in the electoral process but inhibit it to some measurable degree. As Congress has done over the last 70 years or so to address policy issues, the members of Congress should intervene and promote the concept of citizen participation in a more pronounced manner. While some states have election laws that comparatively encourage citizen involvement in the electoral process, other states have laws that clearly could do much more to promote this reality.

Federal elections in the United States need to be more competitive. Incumbents from either major political party in House and Senate elections almost always win, and they typically raise and spend much more money in their campaigns than their challengers.[61] There is only one comprehensive way to remedy this flaw in our electoral system. Professor William Hudson presents a compelling case for the public financing of federal political campaigns:

> The one reform most needed to revitalize our democracy is public financing of election campaigns. The hidden election for campaign funding biases our entire political system in favor of the wealthy and makes a mockery of any notion of equal representation. None of the challenges to democracy discussed in this book will be addressed unless we can end the dominance of big money in our electoral system. The only real solution will be an expanded system of public financing of elections, combined with provision of free airtime for candidates for office. Reforms that simply impose new regulations on campaign financing, such as the 2002 Bipartisan Campaign Reform Act prohibition on soft money, offer only small ameliorations of the system. Nor is relying more on small contributions raised on the Internet, as Obama did in 2008, an adequate solution. As long as candidates are

dependent on private funding for their campaigns, wealthy special interests will find loopholes to get around even the best crafted regulations and will remain a major source of contributions to most candidates. Only full public funding of national campaigns can eliminate the hidden election and permit equal representation, and it must be combined with limits on campaign spending to avoid imposing an extravagant burden on taxpayers. The most logical way to reduce campaign costs would be to provide free media access to major candidates, eliminating the biggest expense of campaigning. Elections are a *public* institution for ensuring the democratic governance; they can succeed as such only with *public* funding and free candidate access to the public airwaves.[62]

It is incumbent upon the members of Congress to pass a substantive public financing law. The history of money and elections in America as delineated in Chapter 5 is painfully clear. Federal officials have done little compared to many European democracies and some American states, including Maine, Vermont, Massachusetts, and Arizona, to regulate the influence of powerful interest groups in elections.[63] Most responses to the challenge of financing House, Senate, and presidential campaigns by Congress have been incremental in nature. The time for significant reform is way past due. In addition, the interpretation that some have of the First Amendment has unfortunate implications for the American political system. Democracy would not exist without freedom of speech and expression. However, no citizens have the right to say or do anything that they please; all citizens belong to a greater community known as American society, and as such, people are held accountable for their speech and actions. If large hordes of cash influence the political process as many Americans believe, than Congress must intervene on behalf of all of us. Law is a balancing of interests; in this instance, the rights of the individual versus the collective rights of general society. In this delicate balance, there is ample room for public financing while preserving individual rights simultaneously.

In the spirit of cooperative federalism, there is another essential reform measure that members of Congress need to address. Legislators in a number of states have frontloaded their primaries during presidential election years so that more attention by the campaigns will be given to their states. Because presidential nominees of both major parties typically have secured the nominations by early March, primaries begin in earnest now in the early part of the year of the election. By March 5, 2008, 37 states had completed their presidential primaries, eight months before the general election in November.[64] There has to be a better way to conduct U.S. primaries, and officials at the National Association of Secretaries of State (NASS) devised a plan in 2008 to conduct rotating regional presidential primaries that merits scrutiny.[65]

In the NASS plan, the country is divided into four regions on a geographical basis: East, South, Midwest, and West. Regional primaries would be held in March, April, May, and June, with the order of the regions rotating every four years. A lottery would be conducted initially to determine the order of the regions the first time that this new system is implemented. Consequently, each region would go first every 16 years. Two states are omitted under the NASS plan: New Hampshire and Iowa, which would retain their leading positions in the presidential selection process so that retail politics rather than costly media-driven campaigns would still exist.[66]

Rather than continue the politics of the past, I would include New Hampshire and Iowa in their respective regions under the NASS plan. While there is a great utility in retail politicking, it is important to treat all the states on an equal basis. Thus, I believe that holding four regional primaries during presidential election years would be a significant improvement over the highly decentralized status quo. Therefore, the groupings are as follows:

East: Connecticut, Delaware, District of Columbia, Maine, Maryland, Massachusetts, New Hampshire, New Jersey, New York, Pennsylvania, Rhode Island, Vermont, and West Virginia (N = 13 states).

Midwest: Illinois, Indiana, Iowa, Kansas, Michigan, Minnesota, Missouri, Nebraska, North Dakota, Ohio, South Dakota, and Wisconsin (N = 12 states).

South: Alabama, Arkansas, Florida, Georgia, Kentucky, Louisiana, Mississippi, North Carolina, Oklahoma, South Carolina, Tennessee, Texas, and Virginia (N = 13 states).

West: Alaska, Arizona, California, Colorado, Hawaii, Idaho, Montana, Nevada, New Mexico, Oregon, Utah, Washington, and Wyoming (N = 13 states).[67]

Having four large primaries during presidential election years would be an exciting reform. Citizens would be much more attentive to the primary season than is presently the case. A significant objective would be to increase voter turnout during the primaries so that more citizens would become engaged during this phase of presidential contests. In conjunction with public financing, our federal elections would be dramatically reformed in a way reminiscent of the changes that were made during the Progressive Era.

Bear in mind that the conception of cooperative federalism articulated in today's context requires an active citizen role in political governance. According to data analysis reports published by the Higher Education Research Institute (HERI) at the University of California, Los Angeles (UCLA), there is reason to be at least cautiously optimistic about this matter, though there is a definitive need for reform as well.[68] Since 1966, college freshmen across the nation have been surveyed about a number of issues. This national longitudinal analysis is the oldest and largest empirical study of higher education in the United States.[69]

The officials at the HERI at UCLA report a revival of political engagement on the part of young people. Almost 86 percent of incoming college students reported that they frequently or occasionally discussed politics in the last year.[70] Almost 36 percent of students indicated that they frequently discussed politics in the last year; this is the highest level garnered since the survey was first administered.[71]

Increases have also occurred in the percentage of students who state that keeping up to date with public affairs is either "essential" or "very important." A record low of 28 percent was recorded in 2000; as of 2008 it has increased to almost 40 percent. In 1966, however, over 60 percent of students surveyed felt that keeping up to date with public affairs was an important personal goal.[72]

There are some encouraging trends with regard to young people and how they perceive the importance of politics in their lives. This positive development needs to continue. Perceptions are so crucial in politics. If young people correctly perceive that politics is important in their lives and in societal terms, they will be more inclined to properly fulfill their roles as citizens in a republican form of government.

Reform Proposal #3: Amend the Federal Constitution

There are at least two fundamental changes that would promote the cause of democracy and citizen participation in our electoral process. Both would require amending the federal Constitution, as congressional statutes and/or state referendums would not suffice. This was demonstrated in a case decided by the U.S. Supreme Court in 1995, *U.S. Term Limits, Inc. v. Thornton*.[73] In 1992, Arkansas voters adopted the 73rd amendment to their state constitution. The amendment in effect limited the terms for members of the U.S. House of Representatives from Arkansas districts to three terms (6 years total) and also limited the terms for members of the U.S. Senate from Arkansas to two terms (12 years total).[74] This state referendum was struck down by the justices of the Supreme Court. Justice John Paul Stevens wrote for the Court's majority and was unequivocal when it came to the issue of altering the federal Constitution:

> We are, however, firmly convinced that allowing the several States to adopt term limits for congressional service would effect a fundamental change in the constitutional framework. Any such change must come not by legislation adopted either by Congress or by an individual State, but rather—as have other important changes in the electoral process—through the Amendment

procedures set forth in Article V. The Framers decided that the qualifications for service in the Congress of the United States be fixed in the Constitution and be uniform throughout the Nation. That decision reflects the Framers' understanding that Members of Congress are chosen by separate constituencies, but that they become, when elected, servants of the people of the United States. They are not merely delegates appointed by separate, sovereign States; they occupy offices that are integral and essential components of a single National Government. In the absence of a properly passed constitutional amendment, allowing individual States to craft their own qualifications for Congress would thus erode the structure envisioned by the Framers, a structure that was designed, in the words of the Preamble to our Constitution, to form a "more perfect Union."[75]

Justice Stevens maintained that the Framers established the requirements for congressional service in Article I (age, citizenship, and residency). The proper way to change these criteria is through a constitutional amendment.

As delineated in Chapter 4, the Framers debated the issue of presidential selection extensively. The option that they ultimately chose, the Electoral College, was a reflection of the context of the times. Direct election was opposed by most of the Framers because they questioned the capability of commoners to select the chief executive. Congressional selection was also dismissed as a viable option, for fear that such a selection mode would violate the principle of checks and balances. The Framers sought to avoid excessive democracy in 1787, but that was over 220 years ago. Democracy has expanded through constitutional amendments, statutory law, as well as judicial decisions. In the world's oldest democracy, it is time to entrust the people to select the U.S. president directly. Citizens in other democracies have this authority as well as responsibility, and Americans do not. This is highly counterintuitive and needs to be remedied without any further delay. Reforming the Electoral College has been debated in the public arena since the early years of the republic. Politically, it is difficult to gain support for changing the status quo, particularly within the more rural states. The focus of the debate, however, tends to be dominated by a perception of the impact that abolishing the Electoral College would have on specific states as well as altering the sacred work of the Framers. On the first point, it should be emphasized that all Americans should have equality when it comes to voting power. Rural states should not have more impact on presidential elections than more urban states. It is simply a matter of fairness. Secondly, the Framers clearly had no consensus on the issue of presidential selection and simply ran out of time in September of 1787 and wished to finalize the Constitution. As such, abolishing the Electoral College in favor of direct election should not be considered taboo; the cause of democracy has advanced on several other fronts when it comes to elections. It is high time that the Electoral College be dissolved. The question of presidential selection is one that the people should resolve without any buffers whatsoever.

Thus, I propose that the Constitution be amended to allow for direct election of the president. The president and vice president would run on the same party ticket, and the ticket that receives the most popular votes would become the president and vice president elect. In this manner, in a very meaningful way all across the nation, every vote would count, and there would be no wasted vote phenomenon as is the case with the Electoral College. If there is concern about the emergence of a consensus candidate, then a threshold of 40.0 (no rounding) percent of the popular vote can be required for victory. Some of America's greatest presidents (e.g., Abraham Lincoln and Woodrow Wilson) were initially elected with about 40 percent of the popular vote.[76] If no candidate garners 40 percent, then a runoff election would be held between the two top vote-getters 30 days henceforth.

Another reform measure focuses on terms of office in the House of Representatives and the Senate. The Framers intended for the House to be closest to the people, as the Framers allowed for direct election of House members with two-year terms. The House remains the most democratic institution at the federal level. Because senators were selected for six-year terms originally by state legislatures, and the president was selected by the Electoral College for four-year terms, the House truly is the "people's house" by comparison. Yet the contemporary Congress is challenged by a number of concrete realities. Political campaigns today, largely waged on television through sound bite commercials, are very expensive. Members in the House in particular, but also in the Senate because senators represent their entire states, are confronted with the realities of the constant campaign, and the race to raise money never ceases.[77] Under the current electoral system, members of Congress spend too much time in the campaign phase, which is obviously an important component of elections, but an insufficient amount of time in the governance phase. With this in mind, I believe that it is time to change the terms of office for members of the U.S. House of Representatives and the U.S. Senate.

The voter turnout data presented in chapter 3 suggests that Americans would welcome having fewer elections, as evidenced by the significantly lower voter turnout during midterm elections as compared to presidential elections. Why not eliminate midterm elections altogether? House terms should be increased to four years by simply changing one word in Article I,

Section 2 which currently reads: "The House of Representatives shall be composed of members chosen every second year by the people of the several states, and the electors in each state shall have the qualifications requisite for electors of the most numerous branch of the state legislature." If members were chosen every fourth year, and elections were held during presidential election years, they would have four-year terms, and more of the electorate would participate by voting in their elections.

The term for senators would subsequently be increased from six to eight years. Currently the Seventeenth Amendment (which changed Article I, Section 3) stipulates that: "The Senate of the United States shall be composed of two Senators from each state, elected by the people thereof, for six years; and each Senator shall have one vote. The electors in each state shall have the qualifications requisite for electors of the most numerous branch of the state legislatures." Yet Article I, Section 3 requires that the Senate be divided into three classes for purposes of elections: "Immediately after they shall be assembled in consequence of the first election, they shall be divided as equally as may be into three classes. The seats of the Senators of the first class shall be vacated at the expiration of the second year, of the second class at the expiration of the fourth year, and the third class at the expiration of the sixth year, so that one third may be chosen every second year."

Thus, a constitutional amendment may stipulate that the Senate be divided into two classes. After the initial election following ratification of an amendment proposal, Senate elections would also coincide with presidential elections. Thus, by way of illustration, all 100 senators could be up for reelection in 2016. This means that citizens would have to choose both U.S. senators representing their state. The two top vote-getters would get the job, so as a result, the major parties would each field two candidates in the general election. Citizens would therefore have four major party candidates from which to select in the November election, along with third-party candidates in pursuance of state law on the subject. Immediately after the election, two classes would be selected. One-half of the Senate (Class I) would be up for reelection in the following federal election (2020) and this would involve one senator from each of the 50 states. In 2024, the senators comprising Class II would be up for reelection, and this, too, would mean that one senator from each of the 50 states would be subject to run for another term of office. As is the case at the present time, if a vacancy occurred, the governor of the state in question could appoint a replacement until a special election could be held, again, in pursuance of state law.

Although congressional terms of office would be increased under this proposal, I would not endorse term limits for federal legislators based on a simple premise articulated by James Madison in *Federalist* No. 53:

A few of the members, as happens in all such assemblies, will possess superior talents; will, by frequent reelections, become members of long standing;
will be thoroughly masters of the public business, and perhaps not unwilling
to avail themselves of those advantages. The greater the proportion of new
members, and the less the information of the bulk of the members the more
apt will they be to fall into the snares that may be laid for them. This remark
is no less applicable to the relation which will subsist between the House of
Representatives and the Senate.[78]

There is no shame in being a skilled legislator with extensive experience
(e.g., Robert Byrd, D-West Virginia). If the people endorse the job that a
House or Senate member is doing, then they reserve the right to keep that
person in office. If, however, they come to the opposite conclusion, then
they can always replace the legislator in question at the next election.

Reform Proposal #4: Embrace the Communitarian Philosophy

Individualism has been part of the American creed at least since the Declaration of Independence was promulgated to the world in 1776.[79] Many
Americans associate democracy with stringent protections of individual
rights. Yet individualism taken too far can undermine democracy, particularly if people isolate themselves and become incapable of empathizing
with one another.[80] As Professor Hudson postulated,

Americans are not shy about asserting their rights. Much of our politics in-
volves individuals or groups entering the public arena to demand recognition or protection of a right. Pro-choice women demand the right to have an
abortion; pro-life women the right to life of the fetus. Smokers claim a right
to smoke; nonsmokers the right to smoke-free air. Labor union members as-
sert their right to strike; businesses their right to hire replacements for strik-
ing workers. "I demand my rights" is perhaps the most commonly heard
phrase in our politics. In the United States, "rights talk" is our predominant
form of political discourse.[81]

While individual rights are of course important in a democracy, they must
be balanced in a reasonable manner with the collective greater common
good. Americans need to remind themselves of the compelling words of a
new president on his inaugural address in 1961:

In the long history of the world, only a few generations have been granted the
role of defending freedom in its hour of maximum danger. I do not shrink
from this responsibility—I welcome it. I do not believe that any of us would
exchange places with any other people or any other generation. The energy,

the faith, the devotion which we bring to this endeavor will light our country and all who serve it. And the glow from that fire can truly light the world.

And so, my fellow Americans, ask not what your country can do for you; ask what you can do for your country.[82]

Simply stated, Americans must learn to balance their emphasis on the protection of individual rights but at the same time be willing to pursue policies that would promote the interests of society at large. In other words, we need to reject the libertarian philosophy as a viable approach to public policy issues.[83]

Using a tax increase proposal by way of illustration, reflect on the words of President Kennedy about a half century ago. Most people, for obvious reasons, are not thrilled with the concept of paying higher taxes because they know that it will generally result in having less disposable income. If the proposed increase in taxes would be utilized for superfluous reasons, then it should be opposed. Governments at all levels are stewards of the public trust and the public treasury.[84] Resources should be utilized in an efficient, effective, and equitable manner. However, the proposed tax increase should not be opposed exclusively because of its perceived impact on the individual and her or his family. Collectively, Americans need to examine the implications of public policy issues in societal terms. If the tax increase would promote a legitimate public enterprise, then it may be worthwhile, even if it entails a measurable burden on individuals. The libertarian philosophy focuses exclusively on the individual and her or his property rights. This is why Professor Hudson contends that the libertarian philosophy, which has been championed in recent decades by such powerful politicians as President Ronald Reagan and President George W. Bush, is illusory in nature. The emphasis of the libertarian philosophy is freedom from government intervention, and it suggests that the United States should be a society where over 300 million individuals pursue their own freedom in a capitalist society free of governmental interference. What libertarians fail to recognize, however, is that while there may be over 300 million citizens in the United States, people are, in reality, interconnected and interdependent with one another. Our collective actions do impact one another, and as a result, public policies should be implemented to promote the interests of greater society and not be predicated upon a perception of reality that may have been more applicable during the Jeffersonian era but does not reflect American society in the modern period.[85]

A communitarian analyzes public policy proposals to determine what the impact may be in broad terms first and foremost; the impact of a statute, executive order, regulation, and/or court order on the individual is secondary in nature. In 2006, then Senator Barack Obama noted in his famous book that:

> I think about America and those who built it. This nation's founders, who somehow rose above petty ambitions and narrow calculations to imagine a nation unfurling across a continent. And those like Lincoln and King, who ultimately laid down their lives in the service of perfecting an imperfect union. And all the faceless, nameless men and women, slaves and soldiers and tailors and butchers, constructing lives for themselves and their children and grandchildren, brick by brick, rail by rail, calloused hand by calloused hand, to fill in the landscape of our collective dreams.[86]

The Framers of the Constitution and early leaders of the republic were all guided by a particular ethos. They were collectively focused on a spirit of public service that emphasized the morality of pursuing the greater common good.[87] Many leaders, and ordinary citizens alike, have been guided by this spirit ever since. In order to reform the electoral process in the United States, leaders and citizens alike will have to be guided by this spirit, which requires all of us to subordinate our individual perspectives and attitudes and prioritize the pursuit of policies that will help our fellow citizens today and those who follow us into the future.

A FINAL WORD

There are many aspects of life in this nation that unites Americans. When citizens are asked to recite the Pledge of Allegiance, or rise for the singing of the national anthem, most comply with pride. Regardless of our ideological and partisan beliefs, were are all collectively democrats and republicans alike. Based on the democratic tradition that formally began in this nation in the Philadelphia Convention and has evolved a great deal since 1787, I have offered some reform proposals to make our electoral system more democratic and more responsive to the collective needs of the people. Inherent in this general paradigm is a requirement for all citizens. In order for the American electoral system to become more democratic, citizens have to become more engaged in public affairs and collectively do their homework. As the ultimate sovereigns in this republican form of government, it is our job to hold our leaders accountable. While there are systematic changes that can do much to promote the noble cause of democracy, there are some simple things that we all could do in the great quest of a more perfect union.

NOTES

CHAPTER 1

1. Alexis de Tocqueville, *Democracy in America* (New York: The Modern Library, 1981), xiii–lviii.

2. Donald W. Rogers (ed.), *Voting and the Spirit of American Democracy: Essays on the History of Voting and Voting Rights in America* (Urbana: University of Illinois Press, 1992), 3.

3. The 13 original colonies were Connecticut, Delaware, Georgia, Maryland, Massachusetts, New Hampshire, New Jersey, New York, North Carolina, Pennsylvania, Rhode Island, South Carolina, and Virginia.

4. Christopher Collier, "The American People as Christian White Men of Property: Suffrage and Elections in Colonial and Early National America," in *Voting and the Spirit of American Democracy: Essays on the History of Voting and Voting Rights in America,* ed. Donald W. Rogers (Urbana: University of Illinois Press, 1992), 19.

5. Independence Hall Association, "Historic Documents: Articles of Confederation," http://www.ushistory.org/documents/confederation.htm (accessed September 10, 2008).

6. Edward J. Larson and Michael P. Winship, *The Constitutional Convention: A Narrative History from the Notes of James Madison* (New York: The Modern Library, 2005), 4–10; other accounts of the Philadelphia Convention include Christopher Collier and James Lincoln Collier, *Decision in Philadelphia: The Constitutional Convention of 1787* (New York: Ballantine Books, 2007) and David O. Stewart, *The Summer of 1787: The Men Who Invented the Constitution* (New York: Simon & Schuster, 2007).

7. Larson and Winship, *The Constitutional Convention*, 8–9.

8. Larson and Winship, *The Constitutional Convention*, 8–9.

9. Independence Hall Association, "Historic Documents."

10. Larson and Winship, *The Constitutional Convention*, 8.

11. Madison outlived all of the other Framers of the Constitution; he passed away in 1836. Congress published his notes in 1840 (Larson and Winship, *The Constitutional Convention*, 162). The legendary Yale historian, Max Farrand, compiled his notes and published them originally in three volumes in *The Records of the Federal Convention of 1787* (1911). A fourth volume was added in 1937. See Max Farrand, *The Records of the Federal Convention of 1787*, rev. ed., 4 vols. (New Haven, CT: Yale University Press, 1966).

12. Not all the Framers formally signed the Constitution. There were a total of 55 delegates from 12 of the 13 states (no delegates were sent from Rhode Island). Thirty-nine Framers signed the document: William Samuel Johnson (CT); Roger Sherman (CT); George Read (DE); Gunning Bedford, Jr. (DE); John Dickinson (DE); Richard Bassett (DE); Jacob Broom (DE); William Few (GA); Abraham Baldwin (GA); James McHenry (MD); Daniel of St. Thomas Jenifer (MD); Daniel Carroll (MD); Nathaniel Gorham (MA); Rufus King (MA); John Langdon (NH); Nicholas Gilman (NH); William Livingston (NJ); David Brearly (NJ); William Paterson (NJ); Jonathan Dayton (NJ); Alexander Hamilton (NY); William Blount (NC); Richard Dobbs Spaight (NC); Hugh Williamson (NC); Benjamin Franklin (PA); Thomas Mifflin (PA); Robert Morris (PA); George Clymer (PA); Thomas Fitzsimons (PA); Jared Ingersoll (PA); James Wilson (PA); Gouverneur Morris (PA); John Rutledge (SC); Charles Cotesworth Pinckney (SC); Charles Pinckney (SC); Pierce Butler (SC); John Blair (VA); James Madison, Jr. (VA); and George Washington (VA). With his signature, the secretary of the convention, William Jackson, was the 40th signer of the U.S. Constitution. Thirteen of the Framers left Philadelphia early and did not sign: Oliver Ellsworth (CT); William Houston (GA); William Pierce (GA); Luther Martin (MD); John Mercer (MD); Caleb Strong (MA); William C. Houston (NJ); John Lansing, Jr. (NY); Robert Yates (NY); William Davie (NC); Alexander Martin (NC); James McClurg (VA); and George Wythe (VA). Three of the Framers refused to sign the document: Elbridge Gerry (MA); George Mason (VA); and Edmund Randolph (VA). For a biographical sketch of all the Framers, review National Archives and Records Administration, "America's Founding Fathers: Delegates to the Constitutional Convention," http://www.archives.gov/exhibits/charters/constitution_founding_fathers.html (accessed September 14, 2008).

13. Larson and Winship, *The Constitutional Convention*, 17.

14. Larson and Winship, *The Constitutional Convention*, 30–33.

15. Sean Wilentz, "Property and Power: Suffrage Reform in the United States, 1787–1860," in *Voting and the Spirit of American Democracy: Essays on the History of Voting and Voting Rights in America*, ed. Donald W. Rogers (Urbana: University of Illinois Press, 1992), 33.

16. George M. Dennison, *The Dorr War: Republicanism on Trial, 1831–1861* (Lexington: University Press of Kentucky, 1976).

17. Glenn M. Linden, *Politics or Principle: Congressional Voting on the Civil War Amendments and Pro-Negro Measures, 1838–69* (Seattle: University of Washington Press, 1976), 3.

18. Roy Morris, Jr., *Fraud of the Century: Rutherford B. Hayes, Samuel Tilden, and the Stolen Election of 1876* (New York: Simon & Schuster, 2003).

19. Avalon Project at Yale Law School, "Voting Rights Act of 1965," http://avalon.yale.edu/20th_century/voting_rights_1965.asp (accessed January 20, 2009).

20. Linden, *Politics or Principle*; William Gillette, *The Right to Vote: Politics and the Passage of the Fifteenth Amendment* (Baltimore: The Johns Hopkins Press, 1969); and John Mabry Mathews, *Legislative and Judicial History of the Fifteenth Amendment* (Baltimore: The Johns Hopkins Press, 1909).

21. Linden, *Politics or Principle*, 4.

22. Linden, *Politics or Principle*, 9–21.

23. Linden, *Politics or Principle*, 4.

24. July 19–20, 1848.

25. National Park Service, "Women's Rights National Historical Park: Declaration of Sentiments," http://www.nps.gov/wori/historyculture/declaration-of-sentiments.htm (accessed October 3, 2008).

26. National Park Service, "Women's Rights National Historical Park."

27. National Park Service, "Women's Rights National Historical Park."

28. Ellen Carol DuBois, "Taking Law into Their Own Hands: Voting Women during Reconstruction," in *Voting and the Spirit of American Democracy: Essays on the History of Voting and Voting Rights in America*, ed. Donald W. Rogers (Urbana: University of Illinois Press, 1992), 66–68.

29. *Bradwell v. Illinois*, 83 U.S. 130 (1873).

30. *Bradwell v. Illinois*.

31. *Bradwell v. Illinois*.

32. Allison Sneider, "Woman Suffrage in Congress: American Expansion and the Politics of Federalism, 1870–1890," in *Votes for Women: The Struggle for Suffrage Revisited*, ed. Jean H. Baker (New York: Oxford University Press, 2002), 77.

33. Rebecca Edwards, "Pioneers at the Polls: Woman Suffrage in the West," in *Votes for Women: The Struggle for Suffrage Revisited*, ed. Jean H. Baker (New York: Oxford University Press, 2002), 90–92.

34. Holly J. McCammon and Karen E. Campbell, "Winning the Vote in the West: The Political Successes of the Women's Suffrage Movements, 1866–1919," *Gender and Society* 15, no. 1 (2001), 77–78.

35. Doug Linder, "Exploring Constitutional Law—Winning the Vote for Women: The 19th Amendment," http://www.law.umkc.edu/faculty/projects/ftrials/conlaw/home.html (accessed October 17, 2008).

36. Ashbrook Center for Public Affairs, "Progressive Platform of 1912," http://www.teachingamericanhistory.org/library/index.asp?document=607 (accessed October 16, 2008).

37. National Election Results, "1912 Presidential General Election Results," http://www.uselectionatlas.org/RESULTS/national.php?f=0&year=1912 (accessed October 19, 2008). Woodrow Wilson won 41.8 percent of the popular vote and

received 435 electoral votes. Theodore Roosevelt received 27.4 percent of the popular vote and tallied 88 electoral votes. He won six states: Pennsylvania (38), South Dakota (5), Michigan (15), Minnesota (12), Washington (7), and California (11). Mr. Wilson received the other two electoral votes from California. William Howard Taft won 23.2 percent of the popular vote and only eight electoral votes as he carried two states: Vermont and Utah. Woodrow Wilson prevailed in all the other states, while the Socialist party candidate, Eugene Debs, received 6 percent of the popular vote but did not win any states.

38. Theodore Roosevelt, *Theodore Roosevelt: An Autobiography* (New York: The Macmillan Company, 1914), 166–167.

39. Samuel John Duncan-Clark, *The Progressive Movement: Its Principles and Its Programme* (Boston: Small, Maynard & Company, 1913), 97.

40. John Allen Gable, *The Bull Moose Years: Theodore Roosevelt and the Progressive Party* (Port Washington, NY: Kennikat Press, 1978), 246–252.

41. Christine A. Lunardini and Thomas J. Knock, "Woodrow Wilson and Woman Suffrage: A New Look," *Political Science Quarterly* 95, no. 4 (1980), 655–671.

42. Sally Hunter Graham, "Woodrow Wilson, Alice Paul, and the Woman Suffrage Movement," *Political Science Quarterly* 98, no. 4 (1983), 665–679.

43. Internet Modern History Sourcebook, "The Passage of the 19th Amendment, 1919–1920 (Articles from *The New York Times*)," http://www.fordham.edu/halsall/mod/1920womensvote.html (accessed October 22, 2008).

44. Graham, "Woodrow Wilson," 669–670.

45. There are no fixed dates to define the time period known as the Progressive Era. However, the decades between 1890–1920 represented a period of substantive changes in American politics, especially with regard to voting and elections. For example, see John D. Buenker and Edward R. Kantowicz (eds.), *Historical Dictionary of the Progressive Era, 1890–1920* (New York: Greenwood Press, 1988). For more information about this time period, see Arthur Mann (ed.), *The Progressive Era: Liberal Renaissance or Liberal Failure?* (New York: Holt, Rinehart and Winston, 1963); Michael McGerr, *A Fierce Discontent: The Rise and Fall of the Progressive Movement in America, 1870–1920* (New York: Free Press, 2003); and George E. Mowry, *The Progressive Era, 1900–1920: The Reform Persuasion* (Washington, D.C.: American Historical Association, 1972).

46. Arthur A. Ekirch, Jr., *Progressivism in America: A Study of the Era from Theodore Roosevelt to Woodrow Wilson* (New York: New Viewpoints, 1974), 112–117.

47. Elizabeth V. Burt, *The Progressive Era: Primary Documents on Events from 1890 to 1914* (Westport, CT: Greenwood Press, 2004), 327–330.

48. Burt, *The Progressive Era,* 328–330.

49. Stephen J. Wayne, *The Road to the White House 2008: The Politics of Presidential Elections,* 8th ed. (Boston: Thomson Higher Education, 2008), 7.

50. Wayne, *The Road to the White House 2008,* 7–8.

51. Wayne, *The Road to the White House 2008,* 8–9.

52. C. E. Fanning, *Selected Articles on Direct Primaries,* 4th ed. (New York: The H. W. Wilson Company, 1918), 2.

53. Fanning, *Selected Articles on Direct Primaries,* 4.

54. Wayne, *The Road to the White House 2008,* 10.

55. Wayne, *The Road to the White House 2008,* 10.

56. Wayne, *The Road to the White House 2008,* 10.

57. Wayne, *The Road to the White House 2008,* 12.

58. Wayne, *The Road to the White House 2008,* 13.

59. Eldon Cobb Evans, *A History of the Australian Ballot System in the United States* (Chicago: The University of Chicago Press, 1917), 6.

60. Evans, *A History,* 10–11.

61. Evans, *A History,* 17–18.

62. David Henry Montgomery, *The Leading Facts of American History* (Boston: The Athenaeum Press, 1899), 377.

63. Evans, *A History,* 70.

64. L. E. Fredman, *The Australian Ballot: The Story of an American Reform* (Lansing: Michigan State University Press, 1968), 134.

65. Daniel A. Smith and Caroline J. Tolbert, *Educated by Initiative: The Effects of Direct Democracy on Citizens and Political Organizations in the American States* (Ann Arbor: The University of Michigan Press, 2004), xi.

66. Smith and Tolbert, *Educated by Initiative,* xii.

67. Smith and Tolbert, *Educated by Initiative,* xii.

68. Smith and Tolbert, *Educated by Initiative,* 9.

69. James Bryce, *The American Commonwealth* (New York: The Macmillan Company, 1906), 324–325. In expressing his criticism for the referendum, Bryce noted that "it is troublesome and costly to take the votes of millions of people over an area so large as that of one of the greater States; much more then is the method difficult to apply in Federal matters. This is the first drawback to the rule of public opinion. The choice of persons for offices is only an indirect and often unsatisfactory way of declaring views of policy, and as the elections at which such choices are made come at fixed intervals, time is lost in waiting for the opportunity of delivering the popular judgment" (p. 499).

70. Smith and Tolbert, *Educated by Initiative,* 4–30.

71. Frederic D. Ogden, *The Poll Tax in the South* (University: University of Alabama Press, 1958), 2.

72. Ogden, *The Poll Tax,* 2.

73. J. Morgan Kousser, *The Shaping of Southern Politics: Suffrage Restrictions and the Establishment of the One-Party South, 1880–1910* (New Haven, CT: Yale University Press, 1974), 64–65.

74. Kousser, *The Shaping of Southern Politics,* 63.

75. *Breedlove v. Suttles,* 302 U.S. 277 (1937).

76. *Breedlove v. Suttles.*

77. The poll tax was still utilized in Alabama, Arkansas, Mississippi, Texas, and Virginia by 1960. James E. Alt, "The Impact of the Voting Rights Act on Black and White Voter Registration in the South," in *Quiet Revolution in the South: The Impact of the Voting Rights Act, 1965–1990,* ed. Chandler Davidson and Bernard Grofman (Princeton, NJ: Princeton University Press, 1994), 356.

78. *Harman v. Forssenius,* 380 U.S. 528 (1965).

79. *Harman v. Forssenius.*

80. Alexander Keyssar, *The Right to Vote: The Contested History of Democracy in the United States* (New York: Basic Books, 2000), 269.

81. *Harper v. Virginia Board of Elections,* 383 U.S. 663 (1966).

82. *Harper v. Virginia Board of Elections.*

83. *Harper v. Virginia Board of Elections.*

84. Keyssar, *The Right to Vote,* 270.

85. Chandler Davidson, "The Recent Evolution of Voting Rights Law Affecting Racial and Language Minorities," in *Quiet Revolution in the South: The Impact of the Voting Rights Act, 1965–1990,* ed. Chandler Davidson and Bernard Grofman (Princeton, NJ: Princeton University Press, 1994), 21–37.

86. Keyssar, *The Right to Vote,* 263–264.

87. Davidson, "The Recent Evolution," 30–31.

88. Davidson, "The Recent Evolution," 30.

89. U.S. Department of Justice, Civil Rights Division, "Introduction to Federal Voting Rights Law," http://www.usdoj.gov/crt/voting/intro/intro.php (accessed January 20, 2009); and Davidson, "The Recent Evolution," 30.

90. *South Carolina v. Katzenbach,* 383 U.S. 301 (1966).

91. *McCulloch v. Maryland,* 17 U.S. 316 (1819).

92. *South Carolina v. Katzenbach.*

93. Davidson, "The Recent Evolution," 30.

94. Public Law 109–246 (July 27, 2006). Fannie Lou Hamer, Rosa Parks, and Coretta Scott King Voting Rights Act Reauthorization and Amendments Act of 2006.

95. Public Law 109–246 (July 27, 2006); and National Commission on the Voting Rights Act, "Voting Rights Act Reauthorized," http://www.votingrightsact.org/reauthorized.html (accessed January 23, 2009).

96. Thomas H. Neale, "The Eighteen Year Old Vote: The Twenty-Sixth Amendment and Subsequent Voting Rates of Newly Enfranchised Age Groups," Congressional Research Service Report No. 83–103 GOV (May 20, 1983), 8, http://digital.library.unt.edu/govdocs/crs/permalink/meta-crs-8805:1 (accessed January 23, 2009).

97. Jenny Diamond Cheng, *Uncovering the Twenty-Sixth Amendment* (Unpublished doctoral dissertation, Department of Political Science, University of Michigan, 2008), 15.

98. Cheng, *Uncovering the Twenty-Sixth Amendment,* 16.

99. Cheng, *Uncovering the Twenty-Sixth Amendment,* 28–151.

100. *Oregon v. Mitchell,* 400 U.S. 112 (1970).

101. *Oregon v. Mitchell.*

102. Cheng, *Uncovering the Twenty-Sixth Amendment,* 25.

103. Cheng, *Uncovering the Twenty-Sixth Amendment,* 25–26.

104. *Oregon v. Mitchell.*

105. Cheng, *Uncovering the Twenty-Sixth Amendment,* 25–26.

106. Neale, "The Eighteen Year Old Vote," 12.

107. Neale, "The Eighteen Year Old Vote," 13–14.

108. Neale, "The Eighteen Year Old Vote," 14.

109. Neale, "The Eighteen Year Old Vote," 15; and Cheng, *Uncovering the Twenty-Sixth Amendment,* 26–27.

110. Federal Voting Assistance Program, "National Voter Registration Act of 1993," http://www.fvap.gov/resources/media/nvralaw.pdf (accessed February 3, 2009).

111. Robert E. DiClerico, *Voting in America: A Reference Handbook* (Santa Barbara, CA: ABC-CLIO, 2004), 289–290.

112. Keyssar, *The Right to Vote,* 151–152.

113. Keyssar, *The Right to Vote,* 152.

114. For a compelling illustration, see William L. Riordon, *Plunkitt of Tammany Hall: A Series of Very Plain Talks on Very Practical Politics* (New York: Dutton, 1963).

115. Keyssar, *The Right to Vote,* 153–156.

116. Keyssar, *The Right to Vote,* 156.

117. Keyssar, *The Right to Vote,* 158.

118. Keyssar, *The Right to Vote,* 159–160.

119. Keyssar, *The Right to Vote,* 159.

120. Keyssar, *The Right to Vote,* 159–162.

121. DiClerico, *Voting in America,* 180.

122. Keyssar, *The Right to Vote,* 315.

123. Keyssar, *The Right to Vote,* 314.

124. U.S. House of Representatives, "U.S. House of Representatives Roll Call Votes 103rd Congress–1st Session, Vote 154 (May 5, 1993)," http://clerk.house.gov/evs/1993/ROLL_100.asp (accessed February 3, 2009).

125. U.S. Senate, "U.S. Senate Roll Call Votes 103rd Congress–1st Session, Vote 118 (May 11, 1993), http://www.senate.gov/legislative/LIS/roll_call_lists/vote_menu_103_1.htm (accessed February 3, 2009).

126. Keyssar, *The Right to Vote,* 314.

127. *Dunn v. Blumstein,* 405 U.S. 330 (1972).

128. *Dunn v. Blumstein.*

129. *Dunn v. Blumstein.*

130. *Dunn v. Blumstein.*

131. *Dunn v. Blumstein.*

132. For a diverse set of analyses of the 2000 presidential election, see Vincent Bugliosi, *The Betrayal of America: How the Supreme Court Undermined the Constitution and Chose our President* (New York: Nation Books, 2001); Alan M. Dershowitz, *Supreme Injustice: How the High Court Hijacked Election 2000* (New York: Oxford University Press, 2001); Brian L. Fife and Geralyn M. Miller, *Political Culture and Voting Systems in the United States: An Examination of the 2000 Presidential Election* (Westport, CT: Praeger, 2002); Douglas Kellner, *Grand Theft 2000: Media Spectacle and a Stolen Election* (Lanham, MD: Rowman & Littlefield Publishers, 2001); and Richard A. Posner, *Breaking the Deadlock: The 2000 Election, the Constitution, and the Courts* (Princeton, NJ: Princeton University Press, 2001).

133. Federal Election Commission, "Help America Vote Act of 2002–Public Law 107–252," http://www.fec.gov/hava/hava.htm (accessed February 4, 2009).

134. U.S. House of Representatives, "U.S. House of Representatives Roll Call Votes 107th Congress–2nd Session, Vote 462 (October 10, 2002)," http://clerk.house.gov/evs/2002/roll462.xml (accessed February 4, 2009).

135. U.S. Senate, "U.S. Senate Roll Call Votes 107th Congress–2nd Session, Vote 238 (October 16, 2002)," http://www.senate.gov/legislative/LIS/roll_call_lists/vote_menu_107_2.htm (accessed February 4, 2009).

136. Federal Election Commission, "Help America Vote Act."

137. *Bush v. Gore,* 531 U.S. 98 (2000).

138. Leslie C. Scott, "Help America Vote Act of 2002: Origins and Impact," in *America Votes!: A Guide to Modern Election Law and Voting Rights,* ed. Benjamin E. Griffith (Chicago: ABA Publishing, 2008), 336–337.

139. Federal Election Commission, "Help America Vote Act."

140. For a discussion of voting systems in the United States, see Fife and Miller, *Political Culture and Voting Systems,* 31–35.

141. Fife and Miller, *Political Culture and Voting Systems,* 65–68.

142. DiClerico, *Voting in America,* 131.

CHAPTER 2

1. 3 U.S.C. 1. It was stipulated by Congress that election day would be the Tuesday after the first Monday in November for the appointment of presidential electors every four years.

2. Library of Congress, "Statutes at Large, 1789–1875," http://memory.loc.gov/ammem/amlaw/lwsllink.html (accessed March 6, 2009).

3. 2 U.S.C. 7.

4. 2 U.S.C. 1.

5. Fife and Miller, *Political Culture and Voting Systems,* 13–14.

6. Because citizens in the District of Columbia were allocated presidential electors in 1961 via the Twenty-Third Amendment, it is treated as a state accordingly.

7. *Dunn v. Blumstein.*

8. North Dakota Secretary of State, "Voter Registration in North Dakota," http://www.nd.gov/sos/electvote/voting/vote-history.html (accessed March 11, 2009).

9. North Dakota Secretary of State, "Voter Registration."

10. Daniel P. Tokaji, "Voter Registration and Election Reform," *William & Mary Bill of Rights* 17, no. 2 (2008), http://ssrn.com/abstract=1292052 (accessed March 15, 2009).

11. Tokaji, "Voter Registration."

12. Tokaji, "Voter Registration."

13. Tokaji, "Voter Registration."

14. Keyssar, *The Right to Vote,* 158.

15. Findlaw, "State-by-State Time Off to Vote Laws," http://www.findlaw.com/voting-rights-law.html (accessed March 19, 2009).

16. Project Vote, "Restoring Voting Rights to Former Felons," http://project vote.org/ (accessed March 19, 2009).

17. Project Vote, "Restoring Voting Rights."

18. Project Vote, "Restoring Voting Rights."

19. Brennan Center for Justice at New York University School of Law, "Voting After Criminal Conviction," http://www.brennancenter.org/ (accessed March 20, 2009).

20. Brennan Center for Justice at New York University School of Law, "Voting After Criminal Conviction."

21. Brennan Center for Justice at New York University School of Law, "Voter Identification," http://www.brennancenter.org/ (accessed March 23, 2009).

22. Project Vote, "Restrictive Voter Identification Requirements," http://pro jectvote.org/ (accessed March 23, 2009).

23. 128 S.Ct. 1610 (2008).

24. *Crawford v. Marion County Election Board.*

25. *Crawford v. Marion County Election Board.*

26. *Crawford v. Marion County Election Board.*

27. *Crawford v. Marion County Election Board.*

28. *Crawford v. Marion County Election Board.*

29. *Crawford v. Marion County Election Board.*

30. *Crawford v. Marion County Election Board.*

31. Daniel Elazar, *American Federalism: A View from the States,* 3rd ed. (New York: Harper & Row, 1984), 2.

32. Elazar, *American Federalism,* 109.

33. Elazar, *American Federalism,* 112.

34. See Farrand, *The Records of the Federal Convention.*

35. Elazar, *American Federalism,* 112.

36. Elazar, *American Federalism,* 115.

37. Elazar, *American Federalism,* 117–118.

38. Elazar, *American Federalism,* 127.

39. Elazar, *American Federalism,* 127.

40. Elazar, *American Federalism,* 130.

41. Elazar, *American Federalism,* 118–119.

42. Elazar, *American Federalism,* 136.

43. Fife and Miller, *Political Culture and Voting Systems,* 26.

CHAPTER 3

1. Peter H. Rossi, Mark W. Lipsey, and Howard E. Freeman, *Evaluation: A Systematic Approach* (Thousand Oaks, CA: Sage, 2004), 203–232.

2. Brian L. Fife, *Desegregation in American Schools: Comparative Intervention Strategies* (New York: Praeger, 1992), 16–25.

3. *Brown v. Board of Education of Topeka, Kansas,* 347 U.S. 483, 98 L.Ed. 873, 74 S.Ct. 686 (1954).

4. The formula for calculating *D* is available in Fife, *Desegregation in American Schools,* 17–18.

5. Fife, *Desegregation in American Schools,* 18–19.

6. Fife, *Desegregation in American Schools,* 20–21.

7. Fife, *Desegregation in American Schools,* 21. For a diverse set of opinions on this measurement issue, see David R. James and Karl E. Taeuber, "Measures of Segregation," in *Sociological Methodology 1985,* ed. Nancy Brandon Tuma (San Francisco: Jossey-Bass, 1985), 1–32; Karl E. Taeuber and Alma F. Taeuber, *Negroes in Cities* (Chicago: Aldine, 1965); Christine H. Rossell, *The Carrot or the Stick for School Desegregation Policy: Magnet Schools or Forced Busing?* (Philadelphia: Temple University Press, 1990); and Patrick Kelly and Will Miller, "Assessing Desegregation Efforts: No 'Best Measure,'" *Public Administration Review* 49, no. 5 (1989), 431–437.

8. Ruy A. Teixeira, *The Disappearing American Voter* (Washington, D.C.: The Brookings Institution, 1992), 5–7.

9. Walter Dean Burnham, "Those High Nineteenth-Century American Voting Turnouts: Fact or Fiction?," *Journal of Interdisciplinary History* 16, no. 4 (1986), 616.

10. Burnham, "Those High Nineteenth-Century," 616.

11. Burnham, "Those High Nineteenth-Century," 616–620.

12. Burnham, "Those High Nineteenth-Century," 620–625.

13. Burnham, "Those High Nineteenth-Century," 625–626.

14. Adjusting for the Fifteenth, Nineteenth, and Twenty-Sixth Amendments, which added African American men; all women; and 18, 19, and 20 year olds; respectively, to the universe in question.

15. Burnham, "Those High Nineteenth-Century," 644.

16. Teixeira, *The Disappearing American Voter,* 6n.

17. U.S. Elections Project, "Voter Turnout," http://elections.gmu.edu/voter_turnout.htm (accessed May 21, 2009).

18. U.S. Elections Project, "Voter Turnout."

19. Michael P. McDonald and Samuel L. Popkin, "The Myth of the Vanishing Voter," *American Political Science Review* 95, no. 4 (2001), 965.

20. Note the title of Teixeira's (1992) book, *The Disappearing American Voter.*

21. McDonald and Popkin, "The Myth of the Vanishing Voter," 963.

22. For example, see Burnham, "Those High Nineteenth-Century"; Walter Dean Burnham, "The Changing Scope of the American Political Universe," *The American Political Science Review* 59, no. 1 (1965), 7–28; Teixeira, *The Disappearing American Voter*; and Paul R. Abramson, John H. Aldrich, and David W. Rohde, *Change and Continuity in the 1996 Elections* (Washington, D.C.: CQ Press, 1998).

23. McDonald and Popkin, "The Myth of the Vanishing Voter," 970.

24. Peter Bruce, "How the Experts Got Voter Turnout Wrong Last Year," *The Public Perspective,* October/November (1997), 39–43.

25. Bruce, "How the Experts," 39.

26. Bruce, "How the Experts," 39.

27. Curtis Gans, "It's Bruce Who Got the Turnout Story Wrong," *The Public Perspective,* October/November (1997), 44–48.

28. Gans, "It's Bruce," 44–45.

29. Gans, "It's Bruce," 46.

30. Curtis Gans, "2004 Primary Turnout Low," March 9, 2004, http://www.fair vote.org/turnout/pressrelease.htm (accessed May 30, 2009).

31. Gans, "2004 Primary Turnout Low."

32. Gans, "2004 Primary Turnout Low."

33. Gans, "2004 Primary Turnout Low."

34. Gans, "2004 Primary Turnout Low."

35. Gans, "2004 Primary Turnout Low."

36. Fife and Miller, *Political Culture and Voting Systems,* 26.

37. For a more in-depth discussion of voter turnout in the American states, see Fife and Miller, *Political Culture and Voting Systems,* 28–31.

38. Freedom House, "*Freedom in the World 2009*: Global Data," http://www. freedomhouse.org/uploads/fiw09/FIW09_Tables&GraphsForWeb.pdf (accessed August 24, 2009).

39. Freedom House, "*Freedom in the World* Methodology Summary," http:// www.freedomhouse.org/uploads/fiw09/FIW_MethodologySummary_ForWeb. pdf (accessed August 25, 2009).

40. The free countries in the *Freedom in the World 2009* survey are: Andorra, Antigua and Barbuda, Argentina, Australia, Austria, Bahamas, Barbados, Belgium, Belize, Benin, Botswana, Brazil, Bulgaria, Canada, Cape Verde, Chile, Costa Rica, Croatia, Cyprus, Czech Republic, Denmark, Dominica, Dominican Republic, El Salvador, Estonia, Finland, France, Germany, Ghana, Greece, Grenada, Guyana, Hungary, Iceland, India, Indonesia, Ireland, Israel, Italy, Jamaica, Japan, Kiribati, Latvia, Lesotho, Liechtenstein, Lithuania, Luxembourg, Mali, Malta, Marshall Islands, Mauritius, Mexico, Micronesia, Monaco, Mongolia, Namibia, Nauru, Netherlands, New Zealand, Norway, Palau, Panama, Peru, Poland, Portugal, Romania, Saint Kitts and Nevis, Saint Lucia, Saint Vincent and Grenadines, Samoa, San Marino, Sao Tome and Principe, Serbia, Slovakia, Slovenia, South Africa, South Korea, Spain, Suriname, Sweden, Switzerland, Taiwan, Trinidad and Tobago, Tuvalu, Ukraine, United Kingdom, United States, Uruguay, and Vanuatu.

41. The partly free countries in the *Freedom in the World 2009* survey are: Albania, Armenia, Bahrain, Bangladesh, Bhutan, Bolivia, Bosnia-Herzegovina, Burkina Faso, Burundi, Central African Republic, Colombia, Comoros, Djibouti, East Timor, Ecuador, Ethiopia, Fiji, Gabon, The Gambia, Georgia, Guatemala, Guinea-Bissau, Haiti, Honduras, Jordan, Kenya, Kuwait, Kyrgyzstan, Lebanon, Liberia, Macedonia, Madagascar, Malawi, Malaysia, Maldives, Moldova, Montenegro, Morocco, Mozambique, Nepal, Nicaragua, Niger, Nigeria, Pakistan, Papua New Guinea, Paraguay, Philippines, Senegal, Seychelles, Sierra Leone, Singapore, Solomon Islands, Sri Lanka, Tanzania, Thailand, Togo, Tonga, Turkey, Uganda, Venezuela, Yemen, and Zambia.

42. The countries categorized as not free in the *Freedom in the World 2009* survey are: Afghanistan, Algeria, Angola, Azerbaijan, Belarus, Brunei, Burma, Cambodia, Cameroon, Chad, China, Congo (Brazzaville), Congo (Kinshasa), Cote d'Ivoire, Cuba, Egypt, Equatorial Guinea, Eritrea, Guinea, Iran, Iraq, Kazakhstan, Laos, Libya, Mauritania, North Korea, Oman, Qatar, Russia, Rwanda, Saudi Arabia, Somalia, Sudan, Swaziland, Syria, Tajikistan, Tunisia, Turkmenistan, United Arab Emirates, Uzbekistan, Vietnam, and Zimbabwe.

43. International Institute for Democracy and Electoral Assistance (International IDEA), "Voter Turnout," http://www.idea.int/vt/ (accessed August 25, 2009).

44. Freedom House, "*Freedom in the World 2009*: Global Data," http://www. freedomhouse.org/uploads/fiw09/FIW09_Tables&GraphsForWeb.pdf (accessed August 24, 2009).

CHAPTER 4

1. Library of Congress, "Today in History: November 4," http://memory.loc. gov/ammem/today/nov04.html (accessed August 31, 2009).

2. Library of Congress, "Today in History: November 4."

3. Fife and Miller, *Political Culture and Voting Systems*.

4. This occurred in 1824 (Democratic-Republican Andrew Jackson garnered more popular votes in a time when the popular vote was not conducted in all the states than another Democratic-Republican rival, John Quincy Adams, but lost the election when the outcome was decided in the U.S. House of Representatives), 1876 (Democrat Samuel Tilden won the popular vote but lost to Republican Rutherford B. Hayes in the Electoral College), 1888 (Grover Cleveland, the incumbent Democratic president, defeated Republican Benjamin Harrison in the popular vote but lost in the Electoral College), and 2000 (Democrat Al Gore defeated George W. Bush by some 540,000 votes but lost in the electoral tally). See George C. Edwards III, *Why the Electoral College is Bad for America* (New Haven, CT: Yale University Press, 2004); Robert A. Dahl, *How Democratic is the American Constitution?* 2nd ed. (New Haven, CT: Yale University Press, 2003); and Fife and Miller, *Political Culture and Voting Systems*.

5. Term limits were established for the president with the ratification of the Twenty-Second Amendment in 1951.

6. For a compelling account of the 1800 presidential election, see Edward J. Larson, *A Magnificent Catastrophe: The Tumultuous Election of 1800, America's First Presidential Campaign* (New York: Free Press, 2007).

7. Stewart, *The Summer of 1787*, 51.

8. Walter J. Oleszek, *Congressional Procedures and the Policy Process*, 8th ed. (Washington, D.C.: CQ Press, 2010).

9. Collier and Collier, *Decision in Philadelphia*, 120–121.

10. Stewart, *The Summer of 1787*, 48–49.

11. Farrand, *The Records of the Federal Convention*, Volume 1: 15–28.

12. Randolph introduced a total of 15 resolutions on this day. See Farrand, *The Records of the Federal Convention*, Volume 1: 20–22.

13. Farrand, *The Records of the Federal Convention,* Volume 1: 21.

14. Farrand, *The Records of the Federal Convention,* Volume 1: 77.

15. Farrand, *The Records of the Federal Convention,* Volume 1: 79.

16. Farrand, *The Records of the Federal Convention,* Volume 1: 77.

17. Farrand, *The Records of the Federal Convention,* Volume 1: 77.

18. Farrand, *The Records of the Federal Convention,* Volume 1: 163.

19. Farrand, *The Records of the Federal Convention,* Volume 1: 174.

20. Farrand, *The Records of the Federal Convention,* Volume 1: 175.

21. Patterson proposed nine resolutions on this day. See Farrand, *The Records of the Federal Convention,* Volume 1: 242–245.

22. Farrand, *The Records of the Federal Convention,* Volume 1: 244.

23. Farrand, *The Records of the Federal Convention,* Volume 1: 242–245.

24. Farrand, *The Records of the Federal Convention,* Volume 2: 22.

25. Farrand, *The Records of the Federal Convention,* Volume 2: 24.

26. Farrand, *The Records of the Federal Convention,* Volume 2: 22.

27. Farrand, *The Records of the Federal Convention,* Volume 2: 24.

28. Farrand, *The Records of the Federal Convention,* Volume 2: 22.

29. Farrand, *The Records of the Federal Convention,* Volume 2: 24.

30. Farrand, *The Records of the Federal Convention,* Volume 2: 23–24.

31. Professor Riker defines heresthetics as an art form where politicians structure the world so that they can prevail on a given issue. See William H. Riker, *The Art of Political Manipulation* (New Haven, CT: Yale University Press, 1986), 34–51; and William H. Riker, "The Heresthetics of Constitution-Making: The Presidency in 1787, with Comments on Determinism and Rational Choice," *American Political Science Review* 78, no. 1 (1984), 1–16.

32. Farrand, *The Records of the Federal Convention,* Volume 2: 30–31.

33. Farrand, *The Records of the Federal Convention,* Volume 2: 29.

34. Farrand, *The Records of the Federal Convention,* Volume 2: 50–51.

35. Farrand, *The Records of the Federal Convention,* Volume 2: 50.

36. Farrand, *The Records of the Federal Convention,* Volume 2: 50.

37. Farrand, *The Records of the Federal Convention,* Volume 2: 50–51.

38. Farrand, *The Records of the Federal Convention,* Volume 2: 50–51.

39. Farrand, *The Records of the Federal Convention,* Volume 2: 84.

40. Farrand, *The Records of the Federal Convention,* Volume 2: 85–86.

41. Farrand, *The Records of the Federal Convention,* Volume 2: 97–98.

42. Edwards, *Why the Electoral College,* 79.

43. Farrand, *The Records of the Federal Convention,* Volume 2: 107–108.

44. Farrand, *The Records of the Federal Convention,* Volume 2: 107–109.

45. Farrand, *The Records of the Federal Convention,* Volume 2: 118.

46. Farrand, *The Records of the Federal Convention,* Volume 2: 116.

47. Farrand, *The Records of the Federal Convention,* Volume 2: 118–120.

48. Collier and Collier, *Decision in Philadelphia,* 227.

49. Collier and Collier, *Decision in Philadelphia,* 252.

50. Farrand, *The Records of the Federal Convention,* Volume 2: 185.

51. Collier and Collier, *Decision in Philadelphia,* 301.

52. Farrand, *The Records of the Federal Convention,* Volume 2: 397–399.

53. Farrand, *The Records of the Federal Convention,* Volume 2: 397–399.

54. Farrand, *The Records of the Federal Convention,* Volume 2: 481.

55. Edwards, *Why the Electoral College,* 79.

56. Farrand, *The Records of the Federal Convention,* Volume 2: 497–498.

57. Stewart, *The Summer of 1787,* 213–216.

58. Farrand, *The Records of the Federal Convention,* Volume 2: 517–520.

59. Farrand, *The Records of the Federal Convention,* Volume 2: 518–520.

60. Farrand, *The Records of the Federal Convention,* Volume 2: 519–520.

61. Farrand, *The Records of the Federal Convention,* Volume 2: 547.

62. Farrand, *The Records of the Federal Convention,* Volume 2: 582.

63. Farrand, *The Records of the Federal Convention,* Volume 2: 641.

64. Dahl, *How Democratic,* 74.

65. David W. Abbott and James P. Levine, *Wrong Winner: The Coming Debacle in the Electoral College* (New York: Praeger, 1991).

66. Fair Vote Presidential Elections Reform Program, "Electoral College: Past Attempts at Reform," http://www.fairvote.org/?page=979 (accessed September 16, 2009).

CHAPTER 5

1. Raymond J. La Raja, *Small Change: Money, Political Parties, and Campaign Finance Reform* (Ann Arbor: The University of Michigan Press, 2008), 15.

2. The data were provided by the Center for Responsive Politics.

3. Center for Responsive Politics, "Banking on Becoming President," http://www.opensecrets.org/pres08/index.php (accessed September 18, 2009).

4. Paul S. Herrnson, Ronald G. Shaiko, and Clyde Wilcox, *The Interest Group Connection: Electioneering, Lobbying, and Policymaking in Washington,* 2nd ed. (Washington, D.C.: CQ Press, 2004).

5. Public Agenda, "Campaign Financing Needs to Be Reformed," in *The Presidential Election Process: Opposing Viewpoints,* ed. Tom Lansford (Detroit: Greenhaven Press, 2008), 73.

6. The data were provided by the Center for Responsive Politics.

7. George C. Edwards III and Stephen J. Wayne, *Presidential Leadership: Politics and Policy Making,* 8th ed. (Boston: Cengage Wadsworth, 2010), 35.

8. American Presidency Project, "Theodore Roosevelt: Fifth Annual Message," http://www.presidency.ucsb.edu/ws/print.php?pid=29546 (accessed October 23, 2009).

9. American Presidency Project, "Theodore Roosevelt."

10. Anthony Corrado, Thomas E. Mann, Daniel R. Ortiz, and Trevor Potter, *The New Campaign Finance Sourcebook* (Washington, D.C.: Brookings Institution Press, 2005), 10–11.

11. Corrado, Mann, Ortiz, and Potter, *The New Campaign,* 12–13.

12. Corrado, Mann, Ortiz, and Potter, *The New Campaign,* 14.

13. Corrado, Mann, Ortiz, and Potter, *The New Campaign,* 14–15.

14. *Newberry v. United States,* 256 U.S. 232 (1921).

15. *Newberry v. United States.*

16. *Newberry v. United States.*

17. *Newberry v. United States.*

18. The justices of the Supreme Court would revisit *Newberry v. United States* in *United States v. Classic,* 313 U.S. 299 (1941).

19. Corrado, Mann, Ortiz, and Potter, *The New Campaign,* 16–17.

20. Corrado, Mann, Ortiz, and Potter, *The New Campaign,* 16–17.

21. *United States v. Classic.*

22. Corrado, Mann, Ortiz, and Potter, *The New Campaign,* 14.

23. Corrado, Mann, Ortiz, and Potter, *The New Campaign,* 18–19.

24. Corrado, Mann, Ortiz, and Potter, *The New Campaign,* 20–21.

25. Corrado, Mann, Ortiz, and Potter, *The New Campaign,* 21.

26. Corrado, Mann, Ortiz, and Potter, *The New Campaign,* 21.

27. Corrado, Mann, Ortiz, and Potter, *The New Campaign,* 22.

28. Corrado, Mann, Ortiz, and Potter, *The New Campaign,* 22.

29. Corrado, Mann, Ortiz, and Potter, *The New Campaign,* 23.

30. Corrado, Mann, Ortiz, and Potter, *The New Campaign,* 23–24.

31. Corrado, Mann, Ortiz, and Potter, *The New Campaign,* 22–23.

32. Corrado, Mann, Ortiz, and Potter, *The New Campaign,* 24.

33. Corrado, Mann, Ortiz, and Potter, *The New Campaign,* 25.

34. *Buckley v. Valeo,* 424 U.S. 1 (1976).

35. *Buckley v. Valeo.*

36. *Buckley v. Valeo.*

37. Corrado, Mann, Ortiz, and Potter, *The New Campaign,* 27.

38. Corrado, Mann, Ortiz, and Potter, *The New Campaign,* 28.

39. Corrado, Mann, Ortiz, and Potter, *The New Campaign,* 29.

40. Corrado, Mann, Ortiz, and Potter, *The New Campaign,* 29–30.

41. Corrado, Mann, Ortiz, and Potter, *The New Campaign,* 36.

42. Corrado, Mann, Ortiz, and Potter, *The New Campaign,* 36–38; and Public Law 107–155 (March 27, 2002). Bipartisan Campaign Reform Act of 2002.

43. Public Law 107–155.

44. Federal Election Commission, "Contribution Limits for 2009–10," http://www.fec.gov/info/contriblimits0910.pdf (accessed November 4, 2009).

45. *McConnell v. Federal Election Commission*, 540 U.S. 93 (2003).

46. *McConnell v. Federal Election Commission.*

CHAPTER 6

1. *The New York Times,* "Field Study: Just How Relevant is Political Science?," http://www.nytimes.com/2009/10/20/books/20poli.html (accessed November 19, 2009).

2. Oliver Wendell Holmes, Jr., "The Path of the Law," *Harvard Law Review* 10, no. 8 (1897), 477–478.

3. Holmes, "The Path of the Law," 478.

4. He gave his speech at the dedication of the Isaac Rich Hall at Boston University School of Law on January 8, 1897.

5. Holmes, "The Path of the Law," 469.

6. Daniel Carroll, John Dickinson, Gouverneur Morris, Robert Morris, and Roger Sherman all signed both the Articles of Confederation and Perpetual Union and the U.S. Constitution.

7. Farrand, *The Records of the Federal Convention*.

8. "Poll Finds Only 33% Can Identify Bill of Rights," *The New York Times*, http://www.nytimes.com/1991/12/15/us/poll-finds-only-33-can-identify-bill-of-rights.html (accessed November 23, 2009).

9. Thurgood Marshall, "Commentary: Reflections on the Bicentennial of the United States Constitution," *Harvard Law Review* 101, no. 1 (1987), 1–5.

10. Marshall, "Commentary," 2.

11. Marshall, "Commentary," 2.

12. Marshall, "Commentary," 5.

13. Stephen Breyer, *Active Liberty: Interpreting our Democratic Constitution* (New York: Alfred A. Knopf, 2005).

14. Breyer, *Active Liberty*.

15. Breyer, *Active Liberty*, 3.

16. Antonin Scalia, *A Matter of Interpretation: Federal Courts and the Law* (Princeton, NJ: Princeton University Press, 1997).

17. Scalia, *A Matter of Interpretation*.

18. Breyer, *Active Liberty*, 117.

19. *McCulloch v. Maryland*.

20. *McCulloch v. Maryland*.

21. *McCulloch v. Maryland*.

22. Jean Edward Smith, *John Marshall: Definer of a Nation* (New York: H. Holt and Co., 1996).

23. *McCulloch v. Maryland*.

24. *McCulloch v. Maryland*.

25. *McCulloch v. Maryland*.

26. Breyer, *Active Liberty*.

27. Avalon Project, "Alien and Sedition Acts," http://avalon.law.yale.edu/18th_century/alien.asp and http://avalon.law.yale.edu/18th_century/sedact.asp (accessed December 14, 2009).

28. Gordon S. Wood, *Empire of Liberty: A History of the Early Republic, 1789–1815* (New York: Oxford University Press, 2009), 239–275.

29. Breyer, *Active Liberty*, 55.

30. Wood, *Empire of Liberty*, 53–94.

31. Farrand, *The Records of the Federal Convention*.

32. Breyer, *Active Liberty*, 56.

33. Samuel D. Warren and Louis D. Brandeis, "The Right to Privacy," *Harvard Law Review* 4, no. 5 (1890), 193–220.

34. U.S. Supreme Court, "Members of the Supreme Court of the United States," http://www.supremecourtus.gov/about/members.pdf (accessed December 19, 2009).

35. Warren and Brandeis, "The Right to Privacy," 193.

36. Breyer, *Active Liberty*, 73.

37. Executive Order 11246–Equal Employment Opportunity (September 24, 1965), http://www.archives.gov/federal-register/codification/executive-order/11246.html (accessed December 20, 2009).

38. The justices reviewed the constitutionality of federal affirmative action programs in 1978 (*Regents of the University of California v. Bakke*, 438 U.S. 265) and 2003 (*Gratz v. Bollinger*, 539 U.S. 244 and *Grutter v. Bollinger*, 539 U.S. 306).

39. Breyer, *Active Liberty*, 83.

40. Breyer, *Active Liberty*, 85.

41. Breyer, *Active Liberty*, 101.

42. Breyer, *Active Liberty*, 102–103.

43. 467 U.S. 837 (1984).

44. Lawrence Baum, *American Courts: Process and Policy*, 6th ed. (Boston: Houghton Mifflin Co., 2008), 2–4.

45. E. E. Schattschneider, *The Semisovereign People: A Realist's View of Democracy in America* (Hinsdale, IL: The Dryden Press, 1960), 141.

46. E. E. Schattschneider, *Party Government* (New York: Rinehart & Company, Inc., 1942), 1.

47. American Political Science Association, Committee on Political Parties, *Toward a More Responsible Two-Party System* (New York: Rinehart & Company, Inc., 1950). The members of the committee included: Thomas S. Barclay (Stanford University), Clarence A. Berdahl (University of Illinois), Hugh A. Bone (University of Washington), Franklin L. Burdette (University of Maryland), Paul T. David (Brookings Institution), Merle Fainsod (Harvard University), Bertram M. Gross (Council of Economic Advisors), E. Allen Helms (Ohio State University), E. M. Kirkpatrick (U.S. Department of State), John W. Lederle (University of Michigan), Fritz Morstein Marx (American University), Louise Overacker (Wellesley College), Howard Penniman (U.S. Department of State), Kirk H. Porter (State University of Iowa), and J. B. Shannon (University of Kentucky). The committee was chaired by E. E. Schattschneider of Wesleyan University.

48. American Political Science Association, *Toward a More Responsible*, v.

49. Morris Fiorina, *Divided Government* (New York: Macmillan, 1992).

50. American Political Science Association, *Toward a More Responsible*, 2.

51. Holmes, "The Path of the Law."

52. Fair Vote Voting and Democracy Research Center, "Primaries: Open and Closed," http://www.archive.fairvote.org/index.php?page=1801 (accessed December 31, 2009). As of February, 2008, the following states have closed primaries: Alaska, Arizona, Colorado, Connecticut, Delaware, District of Columbia, Florida, Hawaii, Iowa, Kansas, Kentucky, Louisiana, Maine, Maryland, Nebraska, Nevada, New Mexico, New York, North Carolina, Oklahoma, Oregon, Pennsylvania, Rhode Island, South Dakota, Utah, and Wyoming.

53. American Rhetoric, "Hubert Humphrey: Democratic National Convention Address, July 14, 1948," http://www.americanrhetoric.com/huberthumprey1948dnc.html (accessed December 19, 2009).

54. American Rhetoric, "Hubert Humphrey."

55. David B. Walker, *The Rebirth of Federalism: Slouching toward Washington*, 2nd ed. (Chappaqua, NY: Chatham House Publishers, 2000).

56. Walker, *The Rebirth of Federalism*.

57. *The Federalist Papers* began to appear in New York city newspapers following the end of the Philadelphia Convention in 1787. They were published under the pseudonym "Publius" and were written by three proponents of ratification of the U.S. Constitution: Alexander Hamilton, James Madison, and John Jay. Alexander Hamilton wrote the majority of the Federalist Papers and later became Secretary of Treasury under President George Washington. James Madison would later serve in the U.S. House of Representatives, as Secretary of State under President Thomas Jefferson, and as the fourth president of the United States. John Jay later became the first chief justice of the U.S. Supreme Court. *The Federalist Papers* are available through the Avalon Project at Yale University Law School: Avalon Project, "*The Federalist Papers*," http://avalon.law.yale.edu/subject_menus/fed.asp (accessed January 5, 2010).

58. Avalon Project, "*The Federalist Papers*: No. 28," http://avalon.law.yale. edu/18th_century/fed28.asp (accessed January 4, 2010).

59. Avalon Project, "*The Federalist Papers*: No. 46," http://avalon.yale.edu/18th_century/fed46.asp (accessed January 4, 2010).

60. In jurisdictions with a relatively small number of voters, the polls could close earlier if all registered voters already cast their ballots.

61. William E. Hudson, *American Democracy in Peril: Eight Challenges to America's Future*, 6th ed. (Washington, D.C.: CQ Press, 2010), 177–178.

62. Hudson, *American Democracy in Peril*, 206–207.

63. Hudson, *American Democracy in Peril*, 207.

64. Center for Responsive Politics, "Primary Calendar," http://opensecrets. org/pres08/calendar.php (accessed January 6, 2010). These states included Iowa (January 3), New Hampshire (January 8), Michigan (January 15), South Carolina (January 19 for the Republicans and January 26 for the Democrats), Florida (January 29), Maine (February 1 for the Republicans and February 10 for the Democrats), Alabama (February 5), Alaska (February 5), Arizona (February 5), Arkansas (February 5), California (February 5), Colorado (February 5), Connecticut (February 5), Delaware (February 5), Georgia (February 5), Illinois (February 5), Kansas (February 5 for the Democrats and February 9 for the Republicans), Massachusetts (February 5), Minnesota (February 5), Missouri (February 5), New Jersey (February 5), New York (February 5), North Dakota (February 5), Oklahoma (February 5), Tennessee (February 5), Utah (February 5), Louisiana (February 9), Washington (February 9), District of Columbia (February 12), Maryland (February 12), Virginia (February 12), Hawaii (February 19), Wisconsin (February 19), Ohio (March 4), Rhode Island (March 4), Texas (March 4), and Vermont (March 4).

65. National Association of Secretaries of State, *The Case for Regional Presidential Primaries in 2012 and Beyond: Report of the NASS Subcommittee on Presiden-*

tial Primaries, February 2008, http://nass.org/index.php?option=com_content& task=view&id=74&Itemid=210 (accessed January 6, 2010).

66. National Association of Secretaries of State, February 2008.

67. National Association of Secretaries of State, February 2008.

68. University of California, Los Angeles (Higher Education Research Institute), "The American Freshman: National Norms for Fall 2008," January 2009, http://www.heri.ucla.edu/PDFs/pubs/briefs/brief-pr012208–08FreshmanNorms. pdf (accessed January 5, 2010).

69. University of California, Los Angeles (Higher Education Research Institute), January 2009.

70. University of California, Los Angeles (Higher Education Research Institute), January 2009.

71. University of California, Los Angeles (Higher Education Research Institute), January 2009.

72. University of California, Los Angeles (Higher Education Research Institute), January 2009.

73. 514 U.S. 779 (1995).

74. *U.S. Term Limits, Inc. v. Thornton* (1995).

75. *U.S. Term Limits, Inc. v. Thornton.*

76. C-SPAN, "C-SPAN 2009 Historians Presidential Leadership Survey," http://www.c-span.org/PresidentialSurvey/presidential-leadership-survey.aspx(accessed January 7, 2010). Abraham Lincoln was ranked the best president in U.S. history in this survey and Woodrow Wilson ranked in the top ten as well (ninth).

77. Paul S. Herrnson, *Congressional Elections: Campaigning at Home and in Washington* 5th ed. (Washington, D.C.: Congressional Quarterly, 2008).

78. Avalon Project, "*The Federalist Papers*: No. 53," http://avalon.law.yale.edu/18th_century/fed53.asp (accessed January 7, 2010).

79. Hudson, *American Democracy in Peril,* 100–133; and William E. Hudson, *The Libertarian Illusion: Ideology, Public Policy and the Assault on the Common Good* (Washington, D.C.: CQ Press, 2008).

80. Tocqueville, *Democracy in America;* and Hudson, *American Democracy in Peril.*

81. Hudson, *American Democracy in Peril,* 121.

82. American Rhetoric, "John F. Kennedy: Inaugural Address (delivered January 20, 1961)," http://www.americanrhetoric.com/speeches/jfkinaugural.htm (accessed January 6, 2010).

83. Hudson, *The Libertarian Illusion;* and Hudson, *American Democracy in Peril.*

84. Roosevelt, *Theodore Roosevelt.*

85. Hudson, *The Libertarian Illusion.*

86. Barack Obama, *The Audacity of Hope: Thoughts on Reclaiming the American Dream* (New York: Crown Publishers, 2006), 361–362.

87. Louis C. Gawthrop, *Public Service and Democracy: Ethical Imperatives for the 21st Century* (New York: Chatham House Publishers, 1998).

BIBLIOGRAPHY

Abbott, David W., and James P. Levine. 1991. *Wrong Winner: The Coming Debacle in the Electoral College.* New York: Praeger.

Abramson, Paul R., John H. Aldrich, and David W. Rohde. 1998. *Change and Continuity in the 1996 Elections.* Washington, D.C.: CQ Press.

Alt, James E. 1994. "The Impact of the Voting Rights Act on Black and White Voter Registration in the South." In *Quiet Revolution in the South: The Impact of the Voting Rights Act, 1965–1990,* ed. Chandler Davidson and Bernard Grofman, 351–377. Princeton, NJ: Princeton University Press.

American Political Science Association, Committee on Political Parties. 1950. *Toward a More Responsible Two-Party System.* New York: Rinehart & Company.

American Presidency Project. 2009. *Theodore Roosevelt: Fifth Annual Message.* Accessed October 23, 2009, from: http://www.presidency/ucsb.edu/ws/print.php?pid=29546.

American Rhetoric. 2009. *Hubert Humphrey: Democratic National Convention Address, July 14, 1948.* Accessed December 19, 2009, from: http://www.americanrhetoric.com/huberthumphrey1948dnc.html.

American Rhetoric. 2010. *John F. Kennedy: Inaugural Address, January 20, 1961.* Accessed January 6, 2010, from: http://www.americanrhetoric.com/speeches/jfkinaugural.htm.

Ashbrook Center for Public Affairs. 2008. *Progressive Platform of 1912.* Accessed October 16, 2008, from: http://www.teachingamericanhistory.org/library/index.asp?document=607.

Avalon Project. 2009. *Alien and Sedition Acts.* Accessed December 14, 2009, from: http://www.avalon.yale.edu/18th_century/alien.asp and http://www.avalon.yale.edu/18th_century/sedact.asp.

Avalon Project. 2009. *Voting Rights Act of 1965.* Accessed January 20, 2009, from: http://avalon.yale.edu/20th_century/voting_rights_1965.asp.

Avalon Project. 2010. *The Federalist Papers.* Accessed January 5, 2010, from: http://avalon.yale.edu/subject_menus/fed.asp.

Avalon Project. 2010. *The Federalist Papers*: No. 28. Accessed January 4, 2010, from: http://avalon.law.yale.edu/18th_century/fed28.asp.

Avalon Project. 2010. *The Federalist Papers*: No. 46. Accessed January 4, 2010, from: http://www.avalon.yale.edu/18th_century/fed46.asp.

Avalon Project. 2010. *The Federalist Papers*: No. 53. Accessed January 7, 2010, from: http://avalon.law.yale.edu/18th_century/fed53.asp.

Baker, Jean H. (ed.). 2002. *Votes for Women: The Struggle for Suffrage Revisited.* New York: Oxford University Press.

Baum, Lawrence. 2008. *American Courts: Process and Policy* (6th ed.). Boston: Houghton Mifflin.

Bradwell v. Illinois, 83 U.S. 130 (1873).

Breedlove v. Suttles, 302 U.S. 277 (1937).

Brennan Center for Justice at New York University School of Law. 2009. *Voter Identification.* Accessed March 23, 2009, from: http://www.brennancenter.org/.

Brennan Center for Justice at New York University School of Law. 2009. *Voting After Criminal Conviction.* Accessed March 20, 2009, from: http://www.brennancenter.org/.

Breyer, Stephen G. 2005. *Active Liberty: Interpreting our Democratic Constitution.* New York: Alfred A. Knopf.

Brown v. Board of Education of Topeka, Kansas, 347 U.S. 483, 98 L.Ed. 873, 74 S.Ct. 686 (1954).

Bruce, Peter. 1997. "How the Experts Got Voter Turnout Wrong Last Year." *The Public Perspective,* October/November, 39–43.

Bryce, James. 1906. *The American Commonwealth.* New York: The Macmillan Company.

Buckley v. Valeo, 424 U.S. 1 (1976).

Buenker, John D., and Edward R. Kantowicz (eds.). 1988. *Historical Dictionary of the Progressive Era.* New York: Greenwood Press.

Bugliosi, Vincent. 2001. *The Betrayal of America: How the Supreme Court Undermined the Constitution and Chose our President.* New York: Nation Books.

Burnham, Walter Dean. 1965. "The Changing Scope of the American Political Universe." *The American Political Science Review* 59(1), 7–28.

Burnham, Walter Dean. 1986. "Those High Nineteenth-Century American Voting Turnouts: Fact or Fiction?" *Journal of Interdisciplinary History* 16(4), 613–644.

Burt, Elizabeth V. 2004. *The Progressive Era: Primary Documents on Events from 1890 to 1914.* Westport, CT: Greenwood Press.

Bush v. Gore, 531 U.S. 98 (2000).

Center for Responsive Politics. 2009. *Banking on Becoming President.* Accessed September 18, 2009, from: http://www.opensecrets.org/pres08/index.php.

Center for Responsive Politics. 2009. *Election Stats.* Accessed October 18, 2009, from: http://www.opensecrets.org/bigpicture/elec_stats.php.

Center for Responsive Politics. 2009. *Presidential Fundraising and Spending, 1976–2008.* Accessed October 18, 2009, from: http://www.opensecrets.org/pres08/totals.php.

Center for Responsive Politics. 2010. Primary Calendar. Accessed January 6, 2010 from: http://www.opensecrets.org/pres08/calendar.php.

Cheng, Jenny Diamond. 2008. Uncovering the Twenty-Sixth Amendment. Unpublished doctoral dissertation, Department of Political Science, University of Michigan. Available at: http://hdl.handle.net/2027.42/58431.

Chevron U.S.A., Inc. v. Natural Resources Defense Council, Inc., 467 U.S. 837 (1984).

Collier, Christopher. 1992. "The American People as Christian White Men of Property: Suffrage and Elections in Colonial and Early National America." In *Voting and the Spirit of American Democracy: Essays on the History of Voting and Voting Rights in America,* ed. Donald W. Rogers, 19–29. Urbana: University of Illinois Press.

Collier, Christopher, and James Lincoln Collier. 2007. *Decision in Philadelphia: The Constitutional Convention of 1787.* New York: Ballantine Books.

Corrado, Anthony, Thomas E. Mann, Daniel R. Ortiz, and Trevor Potter. 2005. *The New Campaign Finance Sourcebook.* Washington, D.C.: Brookings Institution Press.

Crawford v. Marion County Election Board, 128 S.Ct. 1610 (2008).

C-SPAN. 2009. *C-SPAN 2009 Historians Presidential Leadership Survey.* Accessed January 7, 2010, from: http://www.c-span.org/PresidentialSurvey/presidential-leadership-survey.aspx.

Dahl, Robert A. 2003. *How Democratic is the American Constitution* (2nd ed.). New Haven, CT: Yale University Press.

Davidson, Chandler. 1994. "The Recent Evolution of Voting Rights Law Affecting Racial and Language Minorities." In *Quiet Revolution in the South: The Impact of the Voting Rights Act, 1965–1990,* ed. Chandler Davidson and Bernard Grofman, 21–37. Princeton, NJ: Princeton University Press.

Davidson, Chandler, and Bernard Grofman (eds.). 1994. *Quiet Revolution in the South: The Impact of the Voting Rights Act, 1965–1990.* Princeton, NJ: Princeton University Press.

Dennison, George M. 1976. *The Dorr War: Republicanism on Trial, 1831–1861.* Lexington: University Press of Kentucky.

Dershowitz, Alan M. 2001. *Supreme Injustice: How the High Court Hijacked Election 2000.* New York: Oxford University Press.

DiClerico, Robert E. 2004. *Voting in America: A Reference Handbook.* Santa Barbara, CA: ABC-CLIO.

DuBois, Ellen Carol. 1992. "Taking Law into Their Own Hands: Voting Women during Reconstruction." In *Voting and the Spirit of American Democracy: Essays on the History of Voting and Voting Rights in America,* ed. Donald W. Rogers, 66–81. Urbana: University of Illinois Press.

Duncan-Clark, Samuel John. 1913. *The Progressive Movement: Its Principles and Its Programme.* Boston: Small, Maynard & Company.

Dunn v. Blumstein, 405 U.S. 330 (1972).

Early Voting Information Center at Reed College. 2009. *Absentee and Early Voting Laws.* Accessed March 16, 2009, from: http://earlyvoting.net/states/abslaws.php.

Edwards, Rebecca. 2002. "Pioneers at the Polls: Woman Suffrage in the West." In *Votes for Women: The Struggle for Suffrage Revisited,* ed. Jean H. Baker, 90–101. New York: Oxford University Press.

Edwards III, George C. 2004. *Why the Electoral College is Bad for America.* New Haven, CT: Yale University Press.

Edwards III, George C., and Stephen J. Wayne. 2010. *Presidential Leadership: Politics and Policy Making* (8th ed.). Boston: Cengage Wadsworth.

Ekirch, Arthur A., Jr. 1974. *Progressivism in America: A Study of the Era from Theodore Roosevelt to Woodrow Wilson.* New York: New Viewpoints.

Elazar, Daniel J., Jr. 1984. *American Federalism: A View from the States* (3rd ed.). New York: Harper & Row.

Evans, Eldon Cobb. 1917. *A History of the Australian Ballot System in the United States.* Chicago: The University of Chicago Press.

Executive Order 11246–Equal employment opportunity. September 24, 1965. Accessed December 20, 2009, from: http://www.archives.gov/federal-register/codification/executive-order/11246.html.

Fair Vote Presidential Elections Reform Program. 2009. *Electoral College: Past Attempts at Reform.* Accessed September 16, 2009, from: http://www.fairvote.org/?page=979.

Fair Vote Voting and Democracy Research Center. 2009. *Primaries: Open and Closed.* Accessed December 31, 2009, from: http://archive.fairvote.org/index.php?page=1801.

Fanning, C. E. 1918. *Selected Articles on Direct Primaries* (4th ed.). New York: The H. W. Wilson Company.

Farrand, Max (ed.). 1966. *The Records of the Federal Convention of 1787* (vols. I–IV, rev. ed.). New Haven, CT: Yale University Press.

Federal Election Commission. 2009. *Contribution Limits for 2009–10.* Accessed November 4, 2009, from: http://www.fec.gov/info/contriblimits0910.pdf.

Federal Election Commission. 2009. *Help America Vote Act of 2002 (Public Law 107–252).* Accessed February 4, 2009, from: http://www.fec.gov/hava/hava.htm.

Federal Voting Assistance Program. 2009. *National Voter Registration Act of 1993.* Accessed February 3, 2009, from: http://www.fvap.gov/resources/media/nvralaw.pdf.http://www.fvap.gov/resoures/media/nvralaw.pdf

"Field Study: Just How Relevant is Political Science?" October 20, 2009. *The New York Times.* Accessed November 19, 2009, from: http://www.nytimes.com/2009/10/20/books/20poli.html.

Fife, Brian L. 1992. *Desegregation in American Schools: Comparative Intervention Strategies.* New York: Praeger.

Fife, Brian L., and Geralyn M. Miller. 2002. *Political Culture and Voting Systems in the United States: An Examination of the 2000 Presidential Election.* Westport, CT: Praeger.

Findlaw. 2009. *State-by-State Time Off to Vote Laws.* Accessed March 19, 2009, from: http://www.findlaw.com/voting-rights-law.html.

Fiorina, Morris P. 1992. *Divided Government.* New York: Macmillan.

Fredman, L. E. 1968. *The Australian Ballot: The Story of an American Reform.* Lansing: Michigan State University Press.

Freedom House. 2009. *Freedom in the World 2009: Global Data.* Accessed August 24, 2009, from: http://www.freedomhouse.org/uploads/fiw09/FIW09_Tables&GraphsForWeb.pdf.

Freedom House. 2009. *Freedom in the World: Methodology Summary.* Accessed August 25, 2009, from: http://www.freedomhouse.org/uploads/fiw09/FIW_MethodologySummary_ForWeb.pdf.

Gable, John Allen. 1978. *The Bull Moose Years: Theodore Roosevelt and the Progressive Party.* Port Washington, NY: Kennikat Press.

Gans, Curtis. 1997. "It's Bruce Who Got the Turnout Story Wrong." *The Public Perspective* (October/November), 44–48.

Gans, Curtis. 2004. *2004 Primary Turnout Law.* Accessed May 30, 2009, from: http://www.fairvote.org/turnout/pressrelease.htm.

Gawthrop, Louis C. 1998. *Public Service and Democracy: Ethical Imperatives for the 21st Century.* New York: Chatham House Publishers.

Gillette, William. 1969. *The Right to Vote: Politics and the Passage of the Fifteenth Amendment.* Baltimore: The Johns Hopkins Press.

Graham, Sally Hunter. 1983. "Woodrow Wilson, Alice Paul, and the Woman Suffrage Movement." *Political Science Quarterly* 98(4), 665–679.

Gratz v. Bollinger, 539 U.S. 244 (2003).

Griffith, Benjamin E. (ed.). 2008. *America Votes!: A Guide to Modern Election Law and Voting Rights.* Chicago: ABA Publishing.

Grutter v. Bollinger, 539 U.S. 306 (2003).

Harman v. Forssenius, 380 U.S. 528 (1965).

Harper v. Virginia Board of Elections, 383 U.S. 663 (1966).

Herrnson, Paul S. 2008. *Congressional Elections: Campaigning at Home and in Washington* (5th ed.). Washington, D.C.: Congressional Quarterly.

Herrnson, Paul S., Ronald G. Shaiko, and Clyde Wilcox (eds.). 2004. *The Interest Group Connection: Electioneering, Lobbying, and Policymaking in Washington* (2nd ed.). Washington, D.C.: CQ Press.

Holmes, Oliver Wendell, Jr. 1897. "The Path of the Law." *Harvard Law Review* 10(8), 457–478.

Hudson, William E. 2008. *The Libertarian Illusion: Ideology, Public Policy and the Assault on the Common Good.* Washington, D.C.: CQ Press.

Hudson, William E. 2010. *American Democracy in Peril: Eight Challenges to America's Future* (6th ed.). Washington, D.C.: CQ Press.

Independence Hall Association. 2008. *Historic Documents: Articles of Confederation.* Accessed September 10, 2008, from: http://www.ushistory.org/documents/confederation.htm.

International Institute for Democracy and Electoral Assistance (International IDEA). 2009. *Voter Turnout.* Accessed August 25, 2009, from: http://www.idea.int/vt/.

Internet Modern History Sourcebook. 2008. *The Passage of the 19th Amendment, 1919–1920* (Articles from *The New York Times*). Accessed October 22, 2008, from: http://www.fordham.edu/halsall/mod/1920womensvote.html.

James, David R., and Karl E. Taeuber. 1985. "Measures of Segregation." In *Sociological Methodology 1985,* ed. Nancy Brandon Tuma, 1–32. San Francisco: Jossey-Bass.

Kellner, Douglas. 2001. *Grand Theft 2000: Media Spectacle and a Stolen Election.* Lanham, MD: Rowman & Littlefield Publishers.

Kelly, Patrick, and Will Miller. 1989. "Assessing Desegregation Efforts: No 'Best Measure'." *Public Administration Review* 49(5), 431–437.

Keyssar, Alexander. 2000. *The Right to Vote: The Contested History of Democracy in the United States.* New York: Basic Books.

Kousser, J. Morgan. 1974. *The Shaping of Southern Politics: Suffrage Restriction and the Establishment of the One-Party South, 1880–1910.* New Haven, CT: Yale University Press.

Lansford, Tom (ed.). 2008. *The Presidential Election Process: Opposing Viewpoints.* Detroit: Greenhaven Press.

Larson, Edward J. 2007. *A Magnificent Catastrophe: The Tumultuous Election of 1800, America's First Presidential Campaign.* New York: Free Press.

Larson, Edward J., and Michael P. Winship. 2005. *The Constitutional Convention: A Narrative History from the Notes of James Madison.* New York: The Modern Library.

La Raja, Raymond J. 2008. *Small Change: Money, Political Parties, and Campaign Finance Reform.* Ann Arbor: The University of Michigan Press.

League of Women Voters Education Fund. 2009. *Voting in Your State.* Accessed March 11, 2009, from: http://www.vote411.org/bystate.php.

Library of Congress. 2009. *Statutes at Large, 1789–1875.* Accessed March 6, 2009, from: http://memory.loc.gov/ammem/amlaw/lwsllink.html.

Library of Congress. 2009. *Today in History: November 4.* Accessed August 31, 2009, from: http://memory.loc.gov/ammem/today/nov04.html.

Linden, Glenn M. 1976. *Politics or Principle: Congressional Voting on the Civil War Amendments and Pro-Negro Measures, 1838–69.* Seattle: University of Washington Press.

Linder, Doug. 2008. *Exploring Constitutional Law—Winning the Vote for Women: The 19th Amendment.* Accessed October 17, 2008, from: http://www.law.umkc.edu/faculty/projects/ftrials/conlaw/home.html.

Lunardini, Christine A., and Thomas J. Knock. 1980. "Woodrow Wilson and Woman Suffrage: A New Look." *Political Science Quarterly* 95(4), 655–671.

Mann, Arthur (ed.). 1963. *The Progressive Era: Liberal Renaissance or Liberal Failure?* New York: Holt, Rinehart and Winston.

Marshall, Thurgood. 1987. "Commentary: Reflections on the Bicentennial of the United States Constitution." *Harvard Law Review* 101(1), 1–5.

Mathews, John Mabry. 1909. *Legislative and Judicial History of the Fifteenth Amendment*. Baltimore: The Johns Hopkins Press.

McCammon, Holly J., and Karen E. Campbell. 2001. "Winning the Vote in the West: The Political Successes of the Women's Suffrage Movements, 1866–1919." *Gender and Society* 15(1), 55–82.

McConnell v. Federal Election Commission, 540 U.S. 93 (2003).

McCulloch v. Maryland, 17 U.S. 316 (1819).

McDonald, Michael P., and Samuel L. Popkin. 2001. "The Myth of the Vanishing Voter." *American Political Science Review* 95(4), 963–974.

McGerr, Michael. 2003. *A Fierce Discontent: The Rise and Fall of the Progressive Movement in America, 1870–1920*. New York: Free Press.

Montgomery, David Henry. 1899. *The Leading Facts of American History*. Boston: The Athenaeum Press.

Morris, Jr. Roy. 2003. *Fraud of the Century: Rutherford B. Hayes, Samuel Tilden, and the Stolen Election of 1876*. New York: Simon & Schuster.

Mowry, George E. 1972. *The Progressive Era, 1900–20: The Reform Persuasion*. Washington, D.C.: American Historical Association.

National Archives and Records Administration. 2008. *America's Founding Fathers: Delegates to the Constitutional Convention*. Accessed September 14, 2008, from: http://archives.gov/exhibits/charters/constitution_founding_fathers. html.

National Association of Secretaries of State. February 2008. *The Case for Regional Presidential Primaries in 2012 and Beyond: Report of the NASS Subcommittee on Presidential Primaries*. Accessed January 6, 2010, from: http://nass. org/index.php?option=com_content&task=view&id=74&Itemid=210.

National Commission on the Voting Rights Act. July 27, 2006. *Voting Rights Act Reauthorized*. Accessed January 23, 2009, from: http://www.votingrights act.org/reauthorized.html.

National Election Results. 2008. *1912 Presidential General Election Results*. Accessed October 19, 2008, from: http://www.uselectionatlas.org/RESULTS/ national.php?f=0&year=1912.

National Park Service. 2008. *Women's Rights National Historical Park: Declaration of Sentiments*. Accessed October 3, 2008, from: http://www.nps.gov/wori/ historyculture/declaration-of-sentiments.htm.

Neale, Thomas H. 1983. "The Eighteen Year Old Vote: The Twenty-Sixth Amendment and Subsequent Voting Rates of Newly Enfranchised Age Groups." *Congressional Research Service Report Number 83–103 GOV*. Accessed January 23, 2009, from: http://digital.library.unt.edu/govdocs/crs/permalink/ meta-crs-8805:1.

Newberry v. United States, 256 U.S. 232 (1921).

North Dakota Secretary of State. 2009. *Voter Registration in North Dakota*. Accessed March 11, 2009, from: http://nd.gov/sos/electvote/voting/vote-history.html.

Obama, Barack. 2006. *The Audacity of Hope: Thoughts on Reclaiming the American Dream*. New York: Crown Publishers.

Ogden, Frederic D. 1958. *The Poll Tax in the South*. University: University of Alabama Press.

Oleszek, Walter J. 2010. *Congressional Procedures and the Policy Process* (8th ed.). Washington, D.C.: CQ Press.

Oregon v. Mitchell, 400 U.S. 112 (1970).

"Poll Finds Only 33% Can Identify Bill of Rights." December 15, 1991. *The New York Times*. Accessed November 23, 2009, from: http://www.nytimes.com/1991/12/15/us/poll-finds-only-33-can-identify-bill-of-rights.html.

Posner, Richard A. 2001. *Breaking the Deadlock: The 2000 Election, the Constitution, and the Courts*. Princeton, NJ: Princeton University Press.

Project Vote. January 5, 2007. *Restoring Voting Rights to Former Felons. Issues in Election Administration: Policy Brief Number 12*. Accessed March 19, 2009, from: http://projectvote.org.

Project Vote. March 23, 2007. *Restrictive Voter Identification Requirements. Issues in Election Administration: Policy Brief Number 8*. Accessed March 23, 2009, from: http://projectvote.org.

Public Agenda. 2008. "Campaign Financing Needs to Be Reformed." In *The Presidential Election Process: Opposing Viewpoints*, ed. Tom Lansford, 71–78. Detroit: Greenhaven Press.

Public Law 107–155. March 27, 2002. Bipartisan Campaign Reform Act of 2002.

Public Law 109–246. July 27, 2006. Fannie Lou Hamer, Rosa Parks, and Coretta Scott King Voting Rights Act Reauthorization and Amendments Act of 2006.

Regents of the University of California v. Bakke, 438 U.S. 265 (1978).

Riker, William H. 1984. "The Heresthetics of Constitution-Making: The Presidency in 1787, with Comments on Determinism and Rational Choice." *American Political Science Review* 78(1), 1–16.

Riker, William H. 1986. *The Art of Political Manipulation*. New Haven, CT: Yale University Press.

Riordon, William L. 1963. *Plunkitt of Tammany Hall: A series of Very Plain Talks on Very Practical Politics*. New York: Dutton.

Rogers, Donald W. (ed.). 1992. *Voting and the Spirit of American Democracy: Essays on the History of Voting and Voting Rights in America*. Urbana: University of Illinois Press.

Roosevelt, Theodore. 1914. *Theodore Roosevelt: An Autobiography*. New York: The Macmillan Company.

Rossell, Christine H. 1990. *The Carrot or the Stick for School Desegregation Policy: Magnet Schools or Forced Busing?* Philadelphia: Temple University Press.

Rossi, Peter H., Mark W. Lipsey, and Howard E. Freeman. 2004. *Evaluation: A Systematic Approach*. Thousand Oaks, CA: Sage.

Scalia, Antonin. 1997. *A Matter of Interpretation: Federal Courts and the Law*. Princeton, NJ: Princeton University Press.

Schattschneider, E. E. 1942. *Party Government*. New York: Rinehart & Company.

Schattschneider, E. E. 1960. *The Semisovereign People: A Realist's View of Democracy in America*. Hinsdale, IL: The Dryden Press.

Scott, Leslie C. 2008. "Help America Vote Act of 2002: Origins and Impact." In *America Votes!: A Guide to Modern Election Law and Voting Rights,* ed. Benjamin E. Griffith, 335–352. Chicago: ABA Publishing.

Smith, Daniel A., and Caroline J. Tolbert. 2004. *Educated by Initiative: The Effects of Direct Democracy on Citizens and Political Organizations in the American States.* Ann Arbor: University of Michigan Press.

Smith, Jean Edward. 1996. *John Marshall: Definer of a Nation.* New York: H. Holt and Co.

Sneider, Allison. 2002. "Woman Suffrage in Congress: American Expansion and the Politics of Federalism, 1870–1890." In *Votes for Women: The Struggle for Suffrage Revisited,* ed. Jean H. Baker, 77–89. New York: Oxford University Press.

South Carolina v. Katzenbach, 383 U.S. 301 (1966).

Stewart, David O. 2007. *The Summer of 1787: The Men Who Invented the Constitution.* New York: Simon & Schuster.

Taeuber, Karl E., and Alma F. Taeuber. 1965. *Negroes in Cities.* Chicago: Aldine.

Teixeira, Ruy A. 1992. *The Disappearing American Voter.* Washington, D.C.: The Brookings Institution.

Tocqueville, Alexis de. 1981. *Democracy in America.* New York: The Modern Library.

Tokaji, Daniel P. 2008. Voter Registration and Election Reform. *William & Mary Bill of Rights, 17:2.* Accessed March 15, 2009, from: http://ssrn.com/abstract=1292052.

Tuma, Nancy Brandon (ed.). 1985. *Sociological Methodology 1985.* San Francisco: Jossey-Bass.

United States v. Classic, 313 U.S. 299 (1941).

University of California, Los Angeles (Higher Education Research Institute). January, 2009. *The American Freshman: National Norms for Fall 2008.* Accessed January 5, 2010, from: http://www.heri.ucla.edu/PDFs/pubs/briefs/brief-pr 012208–08FreshmanNorms.pdf.

U.S. Census Bureau. 2009. *The 2009 Statistical Abstract.* Elections: Voting-Age Population and Voter Participation. Accessed August 10, 2009, from: http://www.census.gov/compendia/statab/tables/09s0402.pdf.

U.S. Department of Justice, Civil Rights Division. 2009. *Introduction to Federal Voting Rights Laws.* Accessed January 20, 2009, from: http://www.usdoj.gov/crt/voting/intro/intro_b.php.

U.S. Elections Project. 2009. *Voter Turnout.* Accessed May 21, 2009, from: http://elections.gmu.edu/voter_turnout.htm.

U.S. House of Representatives. 2009. U.S. House of Representatives Roll Call Votes 103rd Congress—1st Session (1993). Vote 154 (May 5, 1993). Accessed February 3, 2009, from: http://clerk.house.gov/evs/1993/ROLL_100.asp.

U.S. House of Representatives. 2009. U.S. House of Representatives Roll Call Votes 107th Congress—2nd Session (2002). Vote 462 (October 10, 2002). Accessed February 4, 2009, from: http://clerk.house.gov/evs/2002/roll462.xml.

U.S. Senate. 2009. U.S. Senate Roll Call Votes 103rd Congress—1st Session (1993). Vote 118 (May 11, 1993). Accessed February 3, 2009, from: http://www.senate.gov/legislative/LIS/roll_call_lists/vote_menu_103_1.htm.

U.S. Senate. 2009. U.S. Senate Roll Call Votes 107th Congress—2nd Session (2002). Vote 238 (October 16, 2002). Accessed February 4, 2009, from: http://www.senate.gov/legislative/LIS/roll_call_lists/vote_menu_107_2.htm.

U.S. Supreme Court. 2009. *Members of the Supreme Court of the United States.* Accessed December 19, 2009, from: http://www.supremecourtus.gov/about/members.pdf.

U.S. Term Limits, Inc. v. Thornton, 514 U.S. 779 (1995).

Walker, David B. 2000. *The Rebirth of Federalism: Slouching toward Washington* (2nd ed.). Chappaqua, NY: Chatham House Publishers.

Warren, Samuel D., and Louis D. Brandeis. 1890. "The Right to Privacy." *Harvard Law Review* 4(5), 193–220.

Wayne, Stephen J. 2008. *The Road to the White House 2008: The Politics of Presidential Elections* (8th ed.). Boston: Thomson Higher Education.

Wilentz, Sean. 1992. "Property and Power: Suffrage Reform in the United States: 1787–1860." In *Voting and the Spirit of American Democracy: Essays on the History of Voting and Voting Rights in America,* ed. Donald W. Rogers, 31–41. Urbana: University of Illinois Press.

Wood, Gordon S. 2009. *Empire of Liberty: A History of the Early Republic, 1789–1815.* New York: Oxford University Press.

INDEX

About the Author

BRIAN L. FIFE is professor of public affairs and policy at Indiana University—Purdue University Fort Wayne. He received a bachelor of arts degree in Political Science from the University of Maine and a doctorate in the same discipline from the State University of New York at Binghamton. He is the author of *Desegregation in American Schools, School Desegregation in the Twenty-First Century*, the coeditor of *Higher Education in Transition*, and the coauthor of *Political Culture and Voting Systems in the United States*. He grew up in South Berwick, Maine and now resides in Fort Wayne, Indiana.